THE AGE OF THE
Biplane

THE AGE OF THE
Biplane

CHAZ BOWYER

CRESCENT BOOKS
NEW YORK
A BISON BOOK

Copyright © 1981 by Bison Books Limited

This 1983 edition is published by Crescent Books,
distributed by Crown Publishers, Inc.

Printed in Hong Kong

Library of Congress Cataloging in Publication Data

Bowyer, Chaz.
    The age of the biplane.

    Bibliography: p.
    Includes index.
    1. Biplanes – History. I. Title.
TL684.4.B68 1981   629.133'343   82-17309
ISBN 0-517-39939-3

h g f e d c b a

Front jacket: Christen Eagle II.
Front flap: Rittmeister Manfred Freiherr von Richthofen.
Back jacket: German LVG C VI.
Back flap: Charles Nungesser.
Page 1: A Camel of 70 Squadron, RFC, maneuvering onto the
tail of a Fokker DrI triplane.
Page 2/3: Boeing Stearman Kaydet trainer.
Right: Farman F.22, the 'Horace Farman.'

CONTENTS

Introduction

The age of the biplane, if it is to be defined precisely, is in fact the full gamut of man's successful ventures into the skies via a powered, controllable airplane. It stretches from the earliest pioneering 'hops,' measured meticulously in feet and yards or meters, to the present day when biplanes still retain the allegiance and affection of pure flying enthusiasts of every living generation. Thus to specify a particular span of years as a 'biplane age' is perhaps a misnomer, in that such an era is still in existence, albeit on a much reduced scale.

Nevertheless, the golden age of biplanes is generally accepted as belonging to the years 1903–40. In those years the biplane configuration predominated the aeronautical design scene, years in which man's fertile imagination and inherent genius sought every possible – and no few impossible – avenues in trying to progress the penetration of the upper air. Along that shaky path to perfection was a myriad of blind alleys and diversions, as experiments were made with multiwing aircraft; hence a number of these 'one-off' products are also included herein for comparison and illustration of the progress – or otherwise – seriously attempted. Whether successful or plain farcical, each provided its designers with knowledge, be it beneficial or disastrous. Thus each played its tiny part in the striving toward aeronautical perfection.

This biplane age was relatively brief if placed against a backdrop of human evolution, yet within those few decades truly astonishing progress was made. From the American Wright brothers' first sand-hops at Kill Devil Hill it was to be only 11 years until the opening of national hostilities in Europe in what has since been mistitled the 'Great War.' The following four years provided an impetus to aircraft design and progression which might normally have extended over many more years had the period been one of peace. Not all that progress could be considered to be in man's best interests; war necessitated adaption of the fragile aircraft of the day to the grim task of destruction. Advancement of more useful aeronautical outlets was – indeed, had to be – set aside temporarily. Yet the urgency in keeping pace with enemy aviation brought with it a number of hidden benefits for the airplane's future. It can be said that almost every basic facet of later aviation design was first tried, tested, employed, or at the very least mooted by the close of World War I.

Base-rock experience in constructing and operating aircraft of the smallest and largest sizes, from land and water surfaces, with or without benefit of crew comforts, carrying payloads from a few pounds' weight to several thousands of pounds, by day, by night, in mild or extreme climes – all these and hundreds of minor details in construction and use were built, flown and used during those war years. Much of that accumulated experience was to bear fruit in the post-bellum era when nations reverted to more peaceful exploitation of the airways.

They pointed the path to global transportation of people and goods, led to the ever-escalating piercing of height, speed and distance 'barriers,' and by virtue of the leap in fast communication brought the nations of the world into perilously close contact. With rare exceptions the vast bulk of all these facets was achieved in biplanes.

By 1939 and the reeruption of war in Europe, the biplane configuration was already well on the wane, with the monoplane necessarily replacing its 'elder brother' in the forefront of aeronautical progress. Even so, biplanes were not content merely to fade away, and in several air forces biplanes gave sterling operational service in many guises until at least 1945. Thereafter the biplane virtually retired on its considerable laurels as far as first-line service was concerned. The past 30 years, however, have witnessed an extensive revival of loyalty to the biplane, manifested by an ever-growing surge of enthusiasm for rebuilding, refurbishing or from-scratch constructing of replicas of classic biplane designs of yesteryear, apart from purely sporting fields of aviation activity. This wave of what might be termed nostalgia merely emphasizes the constant thrill to be obtained from flying in an open cockpit, surrounded by canvas-skinned, strutted and interwired multiplanes. It has no parallel in the Plexiglas-cocooned cabin of any modern monoplane, because for sheer ecstasy in flight man needs to be in direct contact with the elements he is challenging – he must feel the winds on his face.

This book then is an unabashed attempt to recall the atmosphere of the 'golden years' of the biplane era; a semihistory with heavy emphasis on the unique appeal of the biplane. In the present age of technically superb yet 'soulless' aircraft, where flying – for a majority of the present generations – has become a packaged, effortless, even boring mode of travel; perhaps this evocation of the age of 'real' flying will give an insight to those who have never been privileged to mount the air in a 'real' airplane.

Chaz Bowyer
Norwich, 1981

Above: The delightful Sopwith Pup entered service in 1916 and has been often described by ex-pilots as the 'perfect flying machine.' Powered by an 80 hp Gnome rotary engine and armed with a single Vickers gun, the Pup did much to restore aerial supremacy for the Allies in 1916–17.

Below: Christen Eagle II, a typical example of a modern aerobatic biplane.

To Emulate the Birds

The fantasy of flight, to be released from the invisible bonds of gravity and mimic the effortless cavorting of the proud eagle or humble sparrow, reaches far back into the unrecorded mists of man's history. Ever a restless species, the human race has always sought answers to the unknown and challenged the apparent limitations of its earthbound experience. Watching with envy the unbounded freedom of birds stirred an ambition in the human breast which was to be frustrated for numberless centuries before the initial triumph of man over his terrestrial-chained environment, until that exhilarating day on a lonely desert flat in America in 1903 when a man took to the air in a vehicle capable of control by the touch of a hand. Until that moment the unceasing longing and striving to conquer the air had been a saga of experimentation and no little courage by a relative handful of visionaries and opportunists, with

would-be 'aeronauts' attempting to achieve flight by means air and gas-filled balloons, fragile gliding structures, kites, mathematically designed constructions of little aesthetic beauty or practicable use. Threaded throughout were the many individual, and usually ill-fated, attempts to literally imitate the birds by attaching wing-like shapes to a human frame.

To specify, or even attempt to identify the first man to fly is impossible; much depends, for example, on individual interpretation of the phrase 'to fly.' Myths and legends can be traced to ancient times crediting Greek, Roman, Egyptian, Persian et al gods with such an ability, while 'bird-men' can be identified in the folklore of virtually every civilization. The earliest British 'flier' may well have been King Bladud, forebear of Shakespeare's King Lear, in the ninth century BC, who died trying to fly with feathered 'wings' from the Temple of Apollo in what is now the city of London; in 1507 one John Damian 'took off' from the ramparts of Stirling Castle in Scotland, intending to fly to France. His immediate plunge to earth produced a shattered thigh, yet he was more fortunate than the majority of individuals through the years who jumped from high places depending on manmade wings to sustain their bodies in air. Thus, from such myths as the Icarus and Daedulus legend and on until the late eighteenth century, visionary men maintained their efforts to achieve flight. In 1783 in France ballooning came on the 'aviation' scene as an alternative means of viewing the earth from above – a form of aeronautics which continues to attract its devotees in the present era. As a form of aerial locomotion, however pleasant, ballooning was nevertheless a blind alley; the flimsy spheres were merely slaves, not masters, of the elements, offering no positive method of control in the contexts of navigation or maneuverability.

Although the Italian genius Leonardo da Vinci may be rightly claimed to have been the first man to use his vast scientific knowledge and experience to investigate the mysteries of

flight, the man internationally acknowledged to have been the true father of aeronautics was a Yorkshire baronet, Sir George Cayley (1773–1857). Cayley's carefully considered experiments and ideas led to a conception of design which thereafter set man on the correct path toward powered, controllable flight. If Cayley's (and several others') ideas and working models were basically sound in theory, all lacked the vital power source – a light, powerful engine to provide the motivation so patently lacking in the human muscle framework. Then, in the late nineteenth century, several individuals independently contributed what may be regarded as the next most significant steps to eventual mastery of the air. In 1876 a German, A N Otto, produced the first truly practical four-stroke gasoline engine, thereby providing an eminently more adaptable power-source potential for aviators than the contemporary wide use of much heavier, steam-driven engine plants. In 1884 an Englishman, Horatio F Phillips, published his model airfoil sections, greatly influencing all future design pioneers. A German engineer, Otto Lilienthal, from 1891 until his death in 1896, designed and built a number of successful hang-gliders, both in monoplane and biplane configurations, in which he personally demonstrated human mastery of the most elementary forms of flying. On the other side of the globe an Australian, Lawrence Hargrave, invented what he termed a 'box kite' in 1893 – an example of an inherently stable flying machine which was to be the basic design of almost all European airplanes of the early twentieth century.

Such men and their fellow pioneers provided the means, methods, ideas and impetus for the future of man-controlled flight, but the accolade for being the first men to achieve controlled, sustained, powered flight in a heavier-than-air machine went to two Americans, Orville and Wilbur Wright. Grandsons of a German immigrant, the Wright brothers were by nature inventive and by 1893 had set up in the business of selling and

Pioneers, from left: Orville and Wilbur Wright, Horace Short and Griffith Brewer at Eastchurch, Isle of Sheppey, on 4 May 1909.

manufacturing bicycles in their hometown of Dayton, Ohio. At this time both men became interested in aviation, mainly through the feats and ideas of Lilienthal. When this pioneer was killed, the Wrights took an even deeper interest in aeronautics, and delved into all available literature and documentation available on the subject. Their approach to aviation was methodical and analytical, patiently proceeding thoroughly from stage to stage by testing and experimenting, and concluding that the basis of successful man-controlled flight must be stability. Having accepted this concept, they then evolved their own method of ensuring complete control in order to

Kittyhawk, 1903. The only photo made of man's first flight in a power-driven, heavier-than-air machine, on 17 December 1903. The airplane, piloted by Orville Wright, has just left its monorail, with Wilbur Wright (at right).

maintain stability in actual flight. In August 1899 the Wrights produced their first glider, a biplane, in which they incorporated their own ideas, including a positive method of flexing (warping) the wing-tips to maintain even flight, and a forward 'elevator.' The following year saw the brothers produce their first man-carrying glider – a machine which can be regarded as the prototype of their later powered aircraft. The next three years became a continuing process of improvement, testing, experimenting – including the construction of a working wind-tunnel in which models were tested and observed – until they were satisfied that they had a perfectly controllable glider. All that was needed now was a suitably light, yet efficient engine to be fitted; a task the brothers undertook on their own account rather than employ any existing engine. Accordingly, the Wrights simplified a normal automobile engine of four water-cooled cylinders in-line, reduced its weight, and finally had a

power plant calculated to produce at least 12 hp at 900 rpm, weighing nearly 180 pounds (or 15 pounds per hp). This drove two propellers – of the Wrights' own design – mounted at the rear and driven by a chain-drive transmission.

On the morning of 17 December 1903, just north of the Kill Devil Sand Hill in Dare County, North Carolina, the first Wright *Flyer* (as the brothers had titled their aircraft) made four brief flights under its own power, with Orville Wright making the first historical flight. In Orville's own words:

'As winter was already set in, we should have postponed our trials (*sic*) to a more favorable season, but for the fact that we were determined, before returning home, to know whether the machine possessed sufficient power to fly, sufficient strength to withstand the shock of landings, and sufficient capacity of control to make flight safe in boisterous winds as well as in calm air. [*All four flights that day took off directly into winds varying from 20 to 22 mph.*] When these points had been definitely established, we at once packed our goods and returned home, knowing that the age of the flying machine had come at last.'

Despite the tremendous significance of the Wright brothers' achievement that day, it was to be several years before they received proper recognition of their success, due mainly to the contemporary lack of national and international communications and media for publicity. In the interim the brothers continued their experiments and trials, improving upon their methods of control and, above all, gaining relatively wide experience in actual flying. Meanwhile, in Europe, development of a true airplane had yet to be achieved; yet by 1905 the Wright brothers' *Flyer III* – the world's first fully practical powered airplane – was offering maneuverability and an all-round performance unequalled by any other form of airplane until at least 1909 (apart from even later Wright designs). If the details of the Wright's achievement were still

unknown in Europe, the brothers' excellent work on gliders by 1903 was known to a few European aviators and greatly influenced the designs produced thereafter, especially in France. Then in 1905, *L'Aerophile*, the organ of the Aero-Club de France, published full data on the Wrights' progress from 1903–05, creating a sensation in European flying circles. The next three years saw the emergence of such pioneer pilot-designers as the Voisin brothers, Ferdinand Ferber, English-born Henry Farman and the little Brazilian Alberto Santos-Dumont, each pressing forward with his individual ideas on airplane design.

With rare exceptions all such airplanes were biplanes, based closely on either the Wright *Flyer* or Hargrave's *Box Kite* structures. In 1907 the Frenchman Louis Bleriot introduced his first monoplane. Among other items later to become standard fitments, it included a control column which, by the use

Bristol Box Kite of the Shuttleworth Collection, Old Warden.

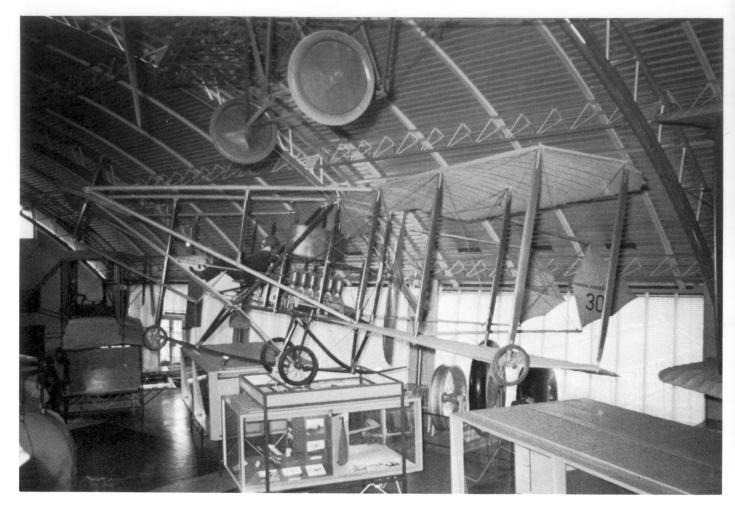

Wright *Flyer* replica, built in 1948 by De Havilland firm
apprentices, which replaced the original 1903 *Flyer* that year
in the Science Museum, London, when the latter was returned
to the United States.

of one hand, operated all major flying control surfaces except
the rudder, which was operated by the feet via a rudder bar.
The monoplane's engine was in front of the pilot – a tractor
type – while its two-wheeled undercarriage incorporated a
shock-absorbing mechanism, with a third wheel under the rear
fuselage. In 1908 Wilbur Wright arrived in France and, commencing on 8 August near Le Mans, spent almost a year giving
superlative flying demonstrations, including duration flights
of up to two and a half hours, and various flights carrying
passengers. Such 'perfection' in flying had never been witnessed in Europe before, and the impression it made on its
spectators was deep and widespread.

The year 1909 can be regarded as possibly the most significant historically in the annals of European aviation, because
in that year occurred several milestones in general progress.
Perhaps the most famous was the crossing of the English Channel on 25 July by Louis Bleriot in his No. XI monoplane. Although
the Channel had first been crossed in a balloon on 1 January
1785, Bleriot's flight was the first airplane crossing – a landmark
in the growing significance of man-controlled flying. A second
occasion was the first international flying meeting held at
Rheims, commencing on 22 August. Though all did not actually
fly, a total of 38 different aircraft participated, and several
distance, speed and duration records were set throughout the
meeting. Perhaps more important – in the context of demonstrating the growing reliability and practicality of the airplane –
was the fact that six machines (four biplanes and two monoplanes) were on offer for sale to the public. Clearly, the airplane was now firmly established in the layman's eye as a
practical mode of transport, albeit still somewhat dangerous

in its application. In Britain the first British subject to fly in an
airplane within the United Kingdom was J T C Moore-Brabazon,
at Leysdown, Isle of Sheppey, at the beginning of May, while
the first British flying meetings took place at Doncaster (15–23
October) and at Blackpool (18–23 October). Each was attended
by a multitude of public spectators; flying had become a
fascination to even the humblest citizen.

With a growing acceptance of the airplane as a viable
machine, it was perhaps inevitable that its use as a military
vehicle should be considered almost from its inception. The
concept of aerial war weaponry was by no means new – now it
was virtually possible. As early as October 1905 the Wright
brothers had offered their 'invention' to the US Government
War Department, though it was to be a further four years before
that bureaucratic body actually purchased a Wright machine.
In 1910 the first tests of weapons from an airborne airplane
were made when Lieutenant Jacob E Fickel, US Army, fired a
rifle at a ground target from the cockpit of a Curtiss biplane on
20 August. On 30 June Glenn Curtiss, the American pioneer
pilot-designer, dropped dummy 'bombs' from a height of 50
feet onto the outline of a battleship, marked by buoys, on Lake
Keuka. The airplane's versatility was also demonstrated on 14
November 1910 when Eugene B Ely flew his Curtiss biplane
off a bows-platform fitted aboard the USS *Birmingham* anchored
in Hampton Roads, Virginia; barely two months later Glenn
Curtiss in his 'hydroairplane' took off, landed, taxied and then
took off again from the waters in San Diego Harbor – a portent of
future naval air power.

Indeed, the years 1910–12 saw an international growth in the
military application of the airplane. On 22 October 1911 an
Italian Bleriot, piloted by Capitano Piazza, flew a reconnaissance flight from Tripoli to Azizia to spy on the opposing
Turkish forces – the first-ever use of an airplane for purely warlike purposes. Ten days later his companion, Lieutenant
Gavotti, dropped (by hand) some 4½-pound grenades on

Above: Orville Wright's aircraft en route to Fort Myer, Virginia, in August 1908, for a series of flying tests for the US Government. On September 17 he crashed, killing a passenger, Lieutenant T Selfridge, in this machine.
Left: Glenn H Curtiss, the pioneer American pilot and designer, at the controls of the machine he built for the 1909 Rheims air meeting, in which he won the James Gordon Bennett Trophy with a speed of 47.04 mph. Curtiss died in July 1930.

(predominantly) and monoplanes, of widely varying design and origin.

The progress in improvement of performance, stability, and reliability continued apace. By 1912 speeds slightly in excess of 100 mph had been achieved, altitude records had surpassed 10,000 feet, distances of more than 200 miles were flown, and durations of flight had been extended to more than eight hours. No small influence in incentive to airplane designers and pilots of the period were the various large money prizes offered by such benefactors as Lord Northcliffe's *Daily Mail* newspaper for specific feats of flying, and the growing popularity of purely aviation sporting contests. In general the period 1912–14 saw relatively large strides in the evolution of the airplane worldwide, yet the pilot was still regarded as something of a phenomenon – a race apart. Individual flying attracted huge crowds of spectators, marvelling at the daring and skill of this new generation of 'supermen.' It was a brief era which produced a host of names destined to become integral with the 'heroic' age of flight, men like Claude Grahame-White, T O M Sopwith, A V Roe, Geoffrey de Havilland, the Farman brothers, Hubert Latham, the Short brothers, the Hon C S Rolls, J W Dunne, Igo Etrich, American-born Samuel Franklin Cody, the colorful winner of the RFC's 1912 Military Trials, and many others of equal repute. If their fame was high, their numbers were surprisingly small. In January 1911, for example, France could

Turkish troops at the Taguira oasis. In Britain that same year, on 1 April, the Balloon Section of the Royal Engineers was extended to become the Air Battalion, RE, which now included an Aeroplane Company possessing nine airplanes initially. In the following year this formation was disbanded and the Royal Flying Corps was born from its ashes. Meanwhile France and Germany had formed military formations which included airplanes – the beginning of an international build-up of aerial military forces. Nevertheless, none of the airplanes within such formations had been designed specifically for military use, but were simply available aircraft pressed into service, mainly with a view to a possible use as purely reconnaissance machines – the aerial equivalent of the traditional cavalry scout. Standardization in 'military' aircraft was still unknown and each nation's air force comprised a motley mixture of biplanes

14

Above: A First Army Wright Type 'C' airplane in the Philippine Islands at Fort McKinley in February 1912. The men are, left to right: Lieutenant H A Darque, Lieutenant C G Chapman, Lieutenant F P Lahm (pilot), Lieutenant P C Rich, Sergeant V L Burge.
Below: The English pioneer, Thomas Octavius Murdock Sopwith ('Tom') born in 1888, in his modified Howard Wright Box Kite, January 1911 – a machine he flew on a demonstration tour in the United States that year.

boast of 353 certified pilots, Great Britain a mere 57, Germany 46, Italy 32 and Belgium 27, while the United States – where airplane flight was first demonstrated successfully – could count only 26 such men. The price of progress by such a tiny community can be illustrated by the fact that, by 1 July 1912, a total of 155 men and three women had been killed in airplane accidents.

By 1912 the general configuration of the airplane was taking definite standard forms. The days of the outlandish and even freakish designs were dwindling fast as the basic requirements for successful flight became accepted as essential. While countries such as France tended to favor the monoplane – doubtless due to the strong influence of such successful aircraft as the Bleriot machines – a bulk of aircraft were biplanes in some shape or form. The biplane offered more lifting surfaces, greater security with its boxed, wire-braced wings and superstructure – direct derivations of either the Wright *Flyers* or Hargrave's *Box Kite*. While, with the golden advantage of hindsight, it is now recognized that the monoplane was to augur the future outline of the airplane, it must be realized that in the 1903–14 years the fragility – relatively – of an airplane construction called for a modicum of in-built safety. Cantilever structures, though envisaged in principle, were still in the earliest, dangerous stages of evolution. The boxed, braced biplane at least provided an illusion of safety and strength of construction:

Such an increase, automatically, in the factors of weight, drag (that is, resistance to the air flow), and sheer bulk inherent in any biplane or other multiplane design was accepted as a necessary evil. Exacerbating the case against the monoplane was a series of (mainly) unexplained fatal accidents in such aircraft which led, temporarily at least, to a ban on the use of single-wing airplanes in certain air services, including the RFC. Although this ban was brief, its psychological effect lingered in the minds of British officialdom for several years, thereby denying fruitful avenues of aeronautical research and delaying advancement along the eventual path to perfection.

Biplanes were also fairly evenly divided in basic standardization during the same period. A majority were of the 'pusher' type, that is, with the engine placed behind the crew nacelle as in the manner of the Wright *Flyer*. By 1912, however, designers such as A V Roe in England, Deperdussin in France, and others were favoring the 'tractor' type whereby the engine was at the front of the fuselage, an inherently more stable and aerodynamically efficient installation than the pusher. By 1914 the tractor type was to be predominant in all new designs, though pushers continued to provide much of the background to the general aviation scene. Indeed, they became necessary during the opening phases of the European War of 1914–18 due to their efficacy in providing a temporary solution to the thorny military problem of carriage of machine guns et al, prior to the introduction of synchronization gears enabling such guns to be operated safely on tractor designs. Exemplifying this particular military problem was the British Vickers No. 18 pusher biplane which was exhibited at the 1913 Olympia Aero Show, optimistically labelled *Destroyer*. Its chief innovation was a Vickers machine gun mounted in the nose of its nacelle, the result of the airplane's Admiralty contract which

Top: The 'miracle' of flight enthralled thousands of public spectators on every occasion, as witnessed by this crowd at London's Wormwood Scrubs on 27 April 1910 when Claude Grahame-White prepared for his second attempt to capture a *Daily Mail* prize for cross-country flying.
Above: Samuel Franklin Cody, a Texas-born American citizen, was paradoxically one of Britain's true pioneers. Here he is seen flying his No. 3 Circuit of Britain 'Cathedral' at Hendon, 1912.

Above: One of Britain's first 'flown cover' airmail letters.
Right: The shape of things to come – a Grahame-White Box Kite, with its pilot well to the fore!
Far right: Alliott Verdon Roe, founder of the famous Avro firm, built his first man-carrying aircraft, the Roe I, in 1907, seen here minus engine at Brooklands. Only the undersurfaces of its wings are cotton covered.
Below: Horace Short (far right), cofounder of the world's first aircraft production firm, with his Short No. 2 biplane at Leysdown, Isle of Sheppey, Kent, in 1909. In this machine J T C Moore-Brabazon became the first resident Englishman to make an officially recognized airplane flight in England, in early 1909; he was awarded the Aero Club of Great Britain's Aviator Certificate No. 1 on 8 March 1910.

called for '. . . a fighting aeroplane armed with a machine gun.' On its first attempt to fly, the *Destroyer* dug its nose straight into the earth – the weight of the gun had proved too much.

Without question the foremost nation in aviation in the four years prior to the outbreak of war in 1914 had been France. French pilots, engines, airplanes and sheer effort had been virtually unchallenged during those years, and the French influence on pioneering aeronautics was evident everywhere in the flying world. By mid-1914, however, this Gallic supremacy was being overtaken by both British and German aviators. In particular, two Germans had outpaced all existing records by August 1914, when Böhm had remained aloft over Johannisthal for 24 hours and 12 minutes, and Ølrich had achieved an altitude record of 25,780 feet. In Britain A V Roe had designed and built the first Avro 504, father of a prodigious line of highly successful biplanes. De Havilland had produced his first BE2 tractor biplane, a reliable and inherently stable machine which, though an excellent flying machine, was to prove almost

disastrous when employed in large quantity for military purposes later. The BE's rigidly stable flight characteristics – considered essential for the pure art of flying – were patently to its disadvantage when called on for combat maneuverability under aerial war conditions. Sopwith had built the remarkable little *Tabloid* single-seater, capable of speeds of 90 mph, and a float version which won the Schneider Trophy Contest of April 1914. Even this performance was easily surpassed by the Farnborough-designed SE4 which emerged in June 1914 and recorded a maximum speed of 135 mph at ground level.

In other avenues of aeronautical achievement, Imperial Russia could rightfully claim to have produced the world's first four-engined airplane. This was the Sikorsky-Lavrov designed *Le Grand* which first flew in May 1913, and from which was developed the successful line of *Ilya Muromets* giant bombers, beginning in December 1913. The latter had four 100 hp engines, wings spanning 113 feet, with a duration of some five hours fully loaded. Another country to pioneer truly big aircraft was Italy, whose Caproni Ca 30 of 1913 set a pattern for a series of huge biplanes and triplanes from 1914 to 1918. Such aerial mammoths were the precursors for an astonishing variety of flying behemoths during the imminent war years. These were aircraft which in their genesis bore the seeds of the post-bellum world's passenger airliners – and no less the instruments of devastating destruction several decades later when strategic bombing became the cornerstone of most air forces' policies.

The eruption of hostilities among the major nations of Europe in August 1914 brought an immediate cessation to all civil flying, as each nation hastily mustered every available airplane for military service. On the eve of war a total of 881 British subjects (overall) had officially qualified for aviator's certificates. Of these, 492 had been members of the British services – 406 commissioned officers and 86 NCOs, petty officers, ratings and 'other ranks' – whose initial training had come via either the RFC schools at Upavon and Netheravon (153 pupils), or at

Far left: A Caudron G.II of French design, a type much used by both British and French services for training.
Center left: Rowland Ding, in the rear cockpit of his Handley Page G/100 at Hendon, May 1914, with Princess Löwenstein-Wertheim as his passenger, prior to a flight to Paris.
Left: The remarkable little Sopwith Tabloid single-seater, first appeared in April 1914 – a conversion of its original two-seat design – and could reach a speed of 92 mph at low level. From it stemmed a line of successful single-seat float machines used by the RNAS during World War I.
Below: Calbraith Perry Rodgers in his modified Wright machine, *Vin Fiz Flyer*, the aircraft he flew from Long Island to Pasadena in 49 hours, then flew on to Long Beach – a total of 4250 miles in 70 hours – in September 1911.

civilian schools – the most significant of which had been the Bristol Company's various schools of ab initio flying instruction. And in the period 1910–14 (August), no less than 54 British subjects had been killed in various forms of airplane accidents. In August 1914 the combined airplane strength of the British RFC and RNAS was officially 270 (excluding seven airships on RNAS charge), but this figure hardly reflected the *operational* capability; the RFC contingent dispatched to France on 13 August comprised just 63 airplanes. Britain's chief ally, France, could only muster 138 aircraft in squadron use at that date, while the common enemy Germany had mobilized a total of nearly 200 aircraft for front-line use. In the United States, incidentally, notwithstanding that nation's neutrality in 1914, the financial budget report dated 8 December 1914 could only acknowledge a total of 11 airplanes in its services.

If the road to ultimate conquest of the air in an airplane had taken unnumbered centuries, the rapid progress from the Wright brothers' initial flights in 1903 to the brink of international war in August 1914 had been truly astonishing. The airplane was now permanently established as a viable vehicle, capable of transgressing manmade national frontiers with ease, and – such is man's readiness to adulterate every new invention to selfish and/or destructive application – a new weapon of death for the armory of the human race. The following four years were to bear awesome witness to that latter capability.

Far left: Designed mainly by Geoffrey de Havilland, the SE2 'high-speed scout' first flew in this form in October 1914, recording a maximum speed of 96 mph. It saw brief operational use in the next few months in France.

Wings of Eagles

The war of 1914–18 is often quoted as a period of great advancement in aeronautics generally and airplane design in particular. While, like in all generalizations, there is an element of truth in such a contention, it is as well to bear in mind the status of the airplane in 1914. It had yet to be regarded as a commercially viable vehicle of any great importance, while its modest use by military and naval forces was of minimum relevance. Hence any hope of governmental financial subsidizing of steady development was unlikely, at least for many years to come in peacetime. A national conflict of arms, however, brought the airplane into sharp focus as the latest possible 'weapon' to be developed.

Thus throughout the war years every government involved had little choice but to make available enormous sums of money and adequate facilities for the production and progression of the flying machine. Under the hammer pressure of wartime urgency it was natural that relatively rapid progress in many facets of aviation could be accomplished on a time-scale much compressed from any similar period of experimentation in a nonwar situation.

From the purist viewpoint of aviation, however, almost all such progress was confined in the narrow ruts of military application only, producing and developing bigger, faster, better-armed aircraft for specific destructive purposes alone. Little thought or time was devoted to the simple progression of efficient aerial transportation – the original concept for the airplane – and the bulk of skill, labor and finance was devoted – necessarily – to enhancing the purely offensive role of any aircraft; hardly any went into such factors as safety, reliability on a long-term basis, or any other vital aspect of peaceful employment. In balance, it is perfectly true that investigation scientifically of such matters as stress, material strength, improved airfoil sections et al aided the eventual postwar airplane designer. Nevertheless, the lion's share of development throughout the war was basically devoted to mere improvement of *existing* designs and ideas, rather than exploitation of entirely fresh avenues of research. Perhaps the greatest exception to this theme was the aero engine. In 1914 engines barely exceeded an output of 100 hp, offering possible altitudes, usually, of less than 10,000 feet at best. By the end of the war engines of 200 hp and 300 hp or more were relatively common, while some 1918 designs were capable of attaining operating

Above right: Dual instruction for an embryo RFC pilot in a Maurice Farman 'Shorthorn' trainer, 1916.
Left: An Albatros C1 two-seater takes off from a German airfield in the winter of 1915–16.
Below: One of the ungainly Voisin bomber designs used extensively by the French in the early years.

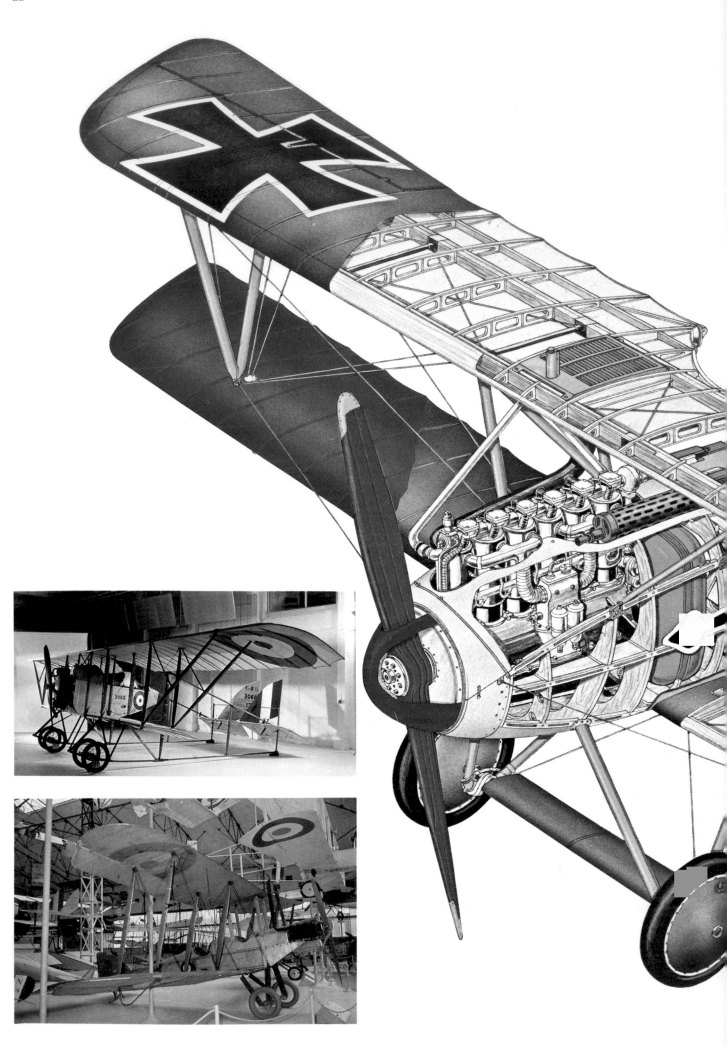

Left: Nieuport 11 Scout – a modern replica, piloted by Joe Pfeiffer, and marked with the Indian's Head insigne of the American-manned *Escadrille Lafayette* of 1916–17.
Below: The Albatros D.Va 'Blitz' flown by Leutnant J von Hippel of Jasta 5 in 1918.
Far left, top: Caudron G.III, in this case an exhibit at the RAF Museum, Hendon, London.
Far left, bottom: The RFC's 'Stability Jane' – nickname for the inherently stable Farnborough-designed BE2c – which equipped many RFC squadrons 1915–16. This example is preserved in the French Musée de l'Air today.

Above: Reconnaissance – the prime role for the airplane throughout 1914–18 – demonstrated by this in-flight view of an Albatros B.II of the Austro-Hungarian air service in early 1917.
Above right: This Morane-Saulnier Type BB two-seat recce aircraft, based on French design, was used by the RFC and the RNAS from 1915–16. The large spinner was called *la casserole* by the French.

altitudes well in excess of 20,000 feet. Actual airplane design, however, tended to lag behind such advancement in power; operational fighters of 1918 could seldom achieve the same speed as the prewar SE4, for merely one example.

The opening phases of the war in Europe saw aircraft employed almost exclusively for what was considered to be their prime military role, reconnaissance of the opposing armies' dispositions and strength along the immediate battle-fronts. The lightness of structure and unreliability of contemporary airplanes precluded any additional loads of pure armament, and most air crews of the period seldom carried aloft anything more lethal than a sharpened pencil with which to jot down details of enemy troops as notes or sketches. If the mechanical means for any direct offensive action against opposing aircraft was absent, the spirit of eager aggression was prevalent among most fliers. Thus it was only a matter of weeks before a number of crews – often without official approval – were carrying aloft a wide selection of personal 'offensive arms' – often no more than a Service rifle or revolver, but occasionally even a humble house-brick or empty wine bottle! Aerial combat per se had yet to be seriously considered in terms of specific armament or even aircraft designed with any such role in mind, yet aerial 'victories' occurred very

Below: Bristol Scout D, No. 8980, an RNAS scout, demonstrates its maneuverability.
Below right: One of the 'great' trainers of World War I was the Curtiss JN4 'Jenny,' illustrated here at an RFC instructional school in Texas, USA, in 1917. After the war 'Jennies' sold for $300, or $500 including flight training.

early in the war, exemplifying the crews' determination to get to grips with the enemy at every opportunity. On 25 August 1914 three aircraft from 2 Squadron, RFC literally forced a German monoplane to land, whereupon its crew abandoned their airplane and escaped, while on the same day a second German aircraft was forced down near Le Quesnoy and captured. Neither 'victory' had entailed the use of guns. The following day, over Galicia, an Austrian two-seater was deliberately rammed by an unarmed Russian Air Service Morane, piloted by Captain Peter Nesterov; both pilots were killed. Then, on 5 October 1914, the first combat victory occurred involving guns, when Corporal Louis Quenault, gunner-observer to Sergeant Joseph Frantz in a Voisin pusher of *Escadrille* VB 24 of the French Air Service, used his machine gun to shoot down a German Aviatik two-seater in flames; its crew, Wilhelm Schlicting and Fritz von Zangen, both perished in their doomed aircraft. The inoffensive airplane had abruptly become a lethal weapon for destruction.

The latter months of 1914 and early weeks of 1915 saw the Allied – British, French, Belgian and Russian – air services almost wholly equipped with biplanes for all purposes; Germany and Austria employed a preponderance of biplanes, intermingled with such pre-1914 designed monoplanes as the Etrich *Taube* (Dove). French-made and designed pushers, such as the Henry and Maurice Farman two-seaters, and the ungainly Voisins, tended to be prominent, partly because of the lack of quantitative production of aircraft as yet in Britain, and in part due to the almost total reliance of British designs on French engines. The main British airplane available in any numbers was the BE2 with a handful of Bristol biplane single- and two-seaters, and occasional examples of the Avro 504 line. Sprinkled haphazardly throughout the few RFC and RNAS units in France and Belgium were also a broad variety of one-off, ex-civilian aircraft hastily pressed into service from August 1914, though these were quickly withdrawn from operations later when in-the-field maintenance proved virtually impossible due to lack of special spares et al. By the spring of 1915 it became fairly common for observers in multiseat aircraft to be

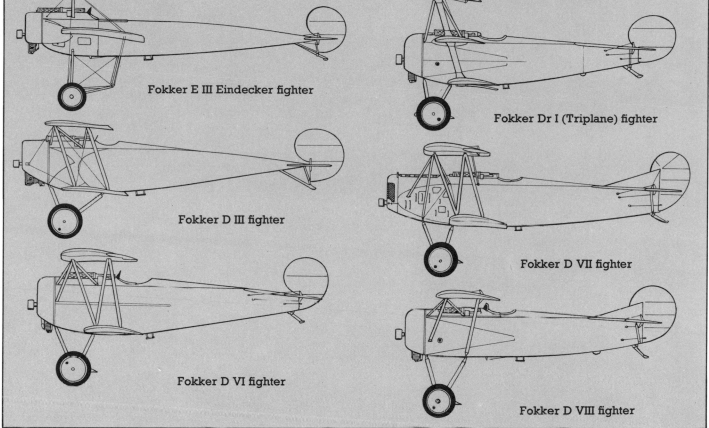

Fokker E III Eindecker fighter

Fokker D III fighter

Fokker D VI fighter

Fokker Dr I (Triplane) fighter

Fokker D VII fighter

Fokker D VIII fighter

provided with some form of defensive armament, usually a repeater carbine or infantry machine gun. Early attempts to arrange bombing sorties led to a variety of lash-up bomb 'carriers' attached under fuselages or wings.

Despite the predominance of biplanes on the world's aviation scene, it fell to two monoplanes to inaugurate the true age of the fighting airplane. On 1 April 1915, after many months of frustrating lack of success and trials, the internationally famed pre-1914 French pilot Roland Garros set out from Dunkerque in a Morane-Saulnier Type L 'parasol' monoplane, carrying two 155-mm bombs in the rear seat, intending to attack a German rail station. Fitted on top of the forward fuselage, directly in front of his cockpit, was a Hotchkiss machine gun, fixed to fire forward along the aircraft's flight-path, *through* the propeller's arc of movement. To obviate the patent danger of occasional bullets striking and shattering the wooden propeller blades, narrow steel wedges had been clamped to both blades in line with the ammunition's trajectory. En route to target Garros encountered a German aircraft, immediately attacked it, and shot it down in flames. On 15 April he shot down a second victim behind German lines, then three days later destroyed an Albatros two-seater near Langemarck. That same afternoon Garros accompanied a bombing raid against Courtrai railway junction and ground fire damaged his aircraft, forcing him to land in German-occupied territory. Though partially destroyed, the remains of his Morane, and its crude form of armament, was quickly studied by engineers of the Fokker aviation firm with a view to possible adaption on one of their own machines.

Finally rejecting Garros's device as too dangerous, the Fokker engineers produced instead a form of mechanically operated 'interrupter' synchronization gun gear – linked via the engine to the propeller shaft – and fitted this to a Fokker M5K monoplane single-seater for trials. On 1 July 1915 Leutnant Kurt Wintgens piloted an armed M5K over French territory and shot down a French Morane – thereby ushering in a period of aerial combat described as the 'Fokker Scourge,' and inci-

dentally confirming starkly that the age of the true flying fighter had arrived. Redesignated as the Fokker E.1 (E = *Eindecker*, or Single-wing) the armed monoplane entered first-line service along the Western Front in France quickly, and in the skilled hands of such pilots as Oswald Boelcke, Max Immelmann, Martin Zander, Max von Mulzer, Otto Parschau, and a dozen others cut a mounting swathe through the ranks of Allied reconnaissance and bomber aircraft during late 1915 and early 1916. The evil reputation of the little Fokker monoplane was, nevertheless, exaggerated; as a war airplane it incorporated several inherent defects, not least of which were its poor climbing ability, a tendency to stall viciously at the start of any quick maneuver, and an inability to maintain a worthy performance at fighting altitude – facets of virtually all contemporary monoplane designs. The biplane's additional wing offered generally superior performance in all these departments of flying, and newly introduced biplane fighters in the Allied air services in early 1916 swiftly dispelled the legendary superiority of the Fokkers.

Within the RFC the arrival on the operational scene of 24 Squadron on 7 February 1916 marked the beginning of the Allied answer to the Fokkers. Commanded by Major Lanoe Hawker, VC, DSO, 24 Squadron RFC was wholly equipped with De Havilland 2 single-seat pusher scouts – the first RFC unit to be so equipped – and on 1 March was joined in France by a second fighter unit, No. 27 Squadron RFC, equipped with Martinsyde G.100 single-seaters. In the ensuing six months these fighters, and further fighting squadrons, attained a form of aerial supremacy over the battle-fronts of France. Other British-designed biplanes to join the fighting at this period included the two-seat Sopwith 1½ Strutter and the ungainly, yet curiously efficient, FE2b pusher aircraft. From the French came a diminutive sesqui-plane scout which was to be employed widely by all Allied air arms from 1916 to early 1918 – the Nieuport Scout. Its introduction in RFC squadrons in mid-1916 was exemplified by its immediately successful use in combat by a 20-year-old Nottingham boy, Albert Ball of 11 and

Sopwith Tabloid

The Sopwith Camel F.1 (D3417) of No. 203 Squadron flown by
R Collishaw, July 1918.

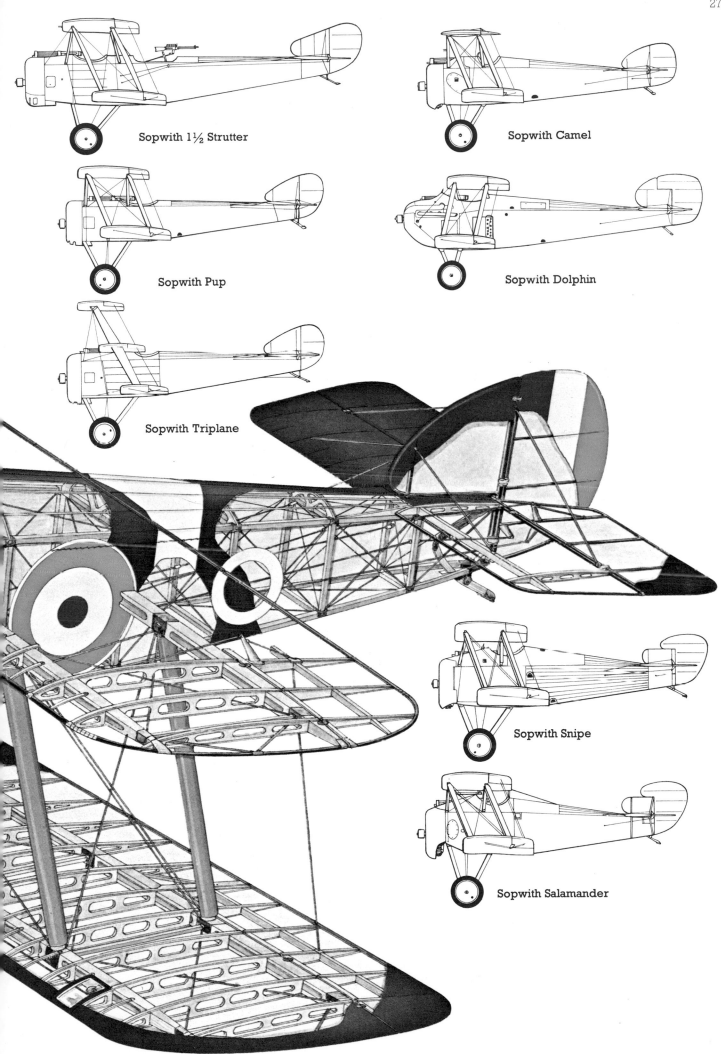

Sopwith 1½ Strutter

Sopwith Camel

Sopwith Pup

Sopwith Dolphin

Sopwith Triplane

Sopwith Snipe

Sopwith Salamander

Left: Flight Lieutenant Lloyd Breadner in his Sopwith Pup *Happy Canuck* at Walmer, Kent, in 1917.
Below left: Refuelling aircraft in World War I was an almost leisurely affair, exemplified here on a De Havilland 6 two-seat trainer at Netheravon on 3 June 1918.

60 Squadrons. By October 1916 Ball had a tally of more than 30 combat victories in Nieuports, and had become the Allied leading fighter pilot. The type also became the fighting mount of a host of future aces, both in British and French squadrons throughout the following year.

If all these fresh Allied fighter types had reestablished aerial superiority in the escalating aerial conflict, such supremacy was short-lived. At the end of August 1916 the German air service formed its first *jagdstaffeln* (literally, hunting squadrons) of fighter pilots, and by mid-September these coordinated fighting teams had begun to make a strong impact of the aerial war. Their successes were due mainly to improved tactical use of completely new fighter designs, chief among which was the biplane Albatros D.I. With its smoothly streamlined, plywood-skinned fuselage, bullet nose, and gracefully curved wings and tail unit, the Albatros had twin synchronized machine guns in front of the pilot – a classic fighter armament installation which was to endure in almost all fighters for the following two decades. Albatros pilots could thus outspeed and outgun any contemporary Allied fighter, and they wrested supremacy from their opponents within weeks. The combined successes of these fresh designs and the tactical use of the new *jagdstaffeln* led to the creation of a total of 37 *Jastas*, almost entirely Albatros-equipped, by the 1917 spring.

If the genesis of aerial combat between fighters tended to

attract the bulk of popular publicity, even giving birth to a continuing legend associated with 'knights of the air,' the most significant development of the wartime aviation progression was undoubtedly that of the bomber. Imperial Russia had already pointed the path to the future with its 1913 *Le Grand* and *Ilya Muromets;* other nations were quick to follow suit in designing multiengined, large aircraft which, after August 1914, became adapted for pure bombing duties. Among the earliest examples projected were the German Ursinus B.1092/14, progenitor of a long line of Gotha bombers which, in 1917–18, raided England, and the British Handley Page 0/100 of 1915, a twin-engined monster with an upper wing spanning 100 feet. While these behemoths were still in the planning and embryo stages, all air services were forced to adapt a variety of designs already in service to become bomb carriers. In the initial absence of specific bomb-carriage devices for aircraft, this usually meant that the tiny 'bombs' – often merely infantry grenades or the like – were taken across the enemy lines and dispensed by an air crew member's good right arm and guesswork aim. It took little time, however, for locally produced fixed bomb racks to be fitted – usually directly under the crews' cockpits, beneath the fuselage – with cable-release by hand once over a target. Aiming was still a matter of individual interpretation of angles and speeds, until the first primitive bombsights began to appear in 1915.

The concept of aerial bombing was realized very early by the French air commanders, and from the beginning weeks of the war employed several *escadrilles* of Voisin pusher bombers in short-range attacks against German targets. In Britain, however, the state of its bombing potential comprised a solitary stockpile of 26 individual 20-pound Hales bombs stored

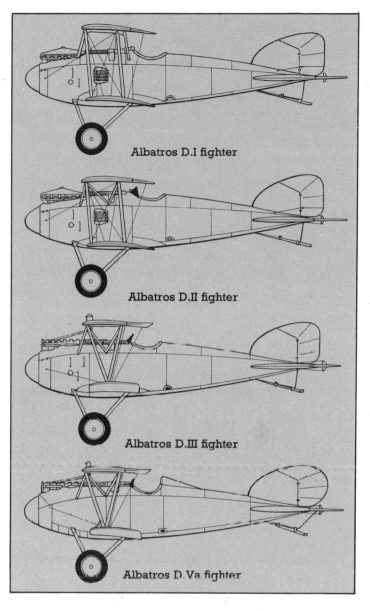

Albatros D.I fighter

Albatros D.II fighter

Albatros D.III fighter

Albatros D.Va fighter

Below: The LFG Roland C.II two-seater of 1916–17, known to its crews as the '*Wahlfisch*' (Whale), showed remarkably clean lines in construction, but was nevertheless tricky to handle, especially during landing.

Above: The Spad S VII, introduced by France in 1916, was, despite its appearance, a single-bay biplane; the inner 'struts' were merely additional strengthening structures. It proved to be one of the classic fighters of World War I, being used by most Allied air services 1916–18, and the mount of many fighter aces. This example is preserved in the Ottawa Museum, Canada.

Above right: By 1917 one of the principal training aircraft of the RFC was the Avro 504, a design that was to continue in RAF service until the early 1930s. This 504K variant now belongs to the Shuttleworth Collection, Old Warden, and is flown regularly.

Opposite, top left: The superbly restored SE5a at Old Warden.

Opposite, top right: Of French design, the Hanriot HD-1 Scout saw wide use in the French, Belgian and Italian air forces. This example at the American Museum at Ottawa, California, bears the wartime personal insigne of the French ace Charles Nungesser.

Right: With equivalent duties to the RE8, the German LVG C VI saw wide service in 1918. This example, 7198/18, was forced down in August 1918 in Allied territory, and since 1966 has been based at Old Warden, still in immaculate flying condition.

Below: The clean, simplified lines of the Fokker D VII are well demonstrated in this example, 8417/18, pictured at RAF Henlow.

Below right: Another meticulously restored veteran is Albatros D.Va, D5390/17, at one time belonging to *Jagdstaffel* 29, and now located at Canberra, Australia.

Opposite, bottom left: The Nieuport 28 Scout saw limited service in 1918, mainly with American pursuit squadrons. This 'rebuild' belonged to Paul Mantz at the time this view was photographed.

Opposite, bottom right: One of the war's doughty workhorses was the British RE8 two-seat reconnaissance and 'spotter' (for the artillery) design of 1917–18. Nicknamed the 'Harry Tate' after a popular contemporary music hall comedian, the RE8 was ill-fitted for pure combat situations. This example, part-stripped, is part of the Imperial War Museum's collection based at Duxford aerodrome, Cambridgeshire, at present.

Above: Albert Ball, VC, in SE5, A4850 of 56 Squadron, RFC at London Colney in late March 1917.
Above right: Nieuport Scout, A126, a fighter flown by Albert Ball, VC, when serving with 11 Squadron, RFC in 1916. A single Lewis gun was mounted above the upper wing.

at RNAS Eastchurch on the Isle of Sheppey. In Italy the authorities had already expressed approval of bombing as a ploy of offensive operations, and such designs as the Caproni Ca-2 were in action from 1915 against Austro-Hungarian objectives. On the German side Ursinus's twin-engined design, the B.1092/14, saw limited active service in 1914, and a much modified and improved version, now titled Gotha G.1, emerged in July 1915. Even then its chief use was as a tactical support aircraft for ground operations, and the exclusive use of later

Gotha designs for bombing only really came from mid-1916. It was not until mid-1917 before the first all-Gotha force was able to commence a planned strategic bombing offensive against English targets. The principles of strategic aerial bombing – a concept initially propounded by a German major, Wilhelm Siegert – were vaguely understood by certain British and French air staff. They were first translated into practical terms with the formation of No. 3 Wing RNAS in May 1916, a combined Anglo-French force of bombers which, after prolonged difficulties in equipment, began operations from Luxeuil in July 1916. Sorties continued at spasmodic intervals until April 1917 when the Wing was disbanded, but included the first ever operations by Britain's Handley Page 0/100 'heavies' – the first of these being flown on 16/17 March 1917. The results achieved by these pioneering crews were not

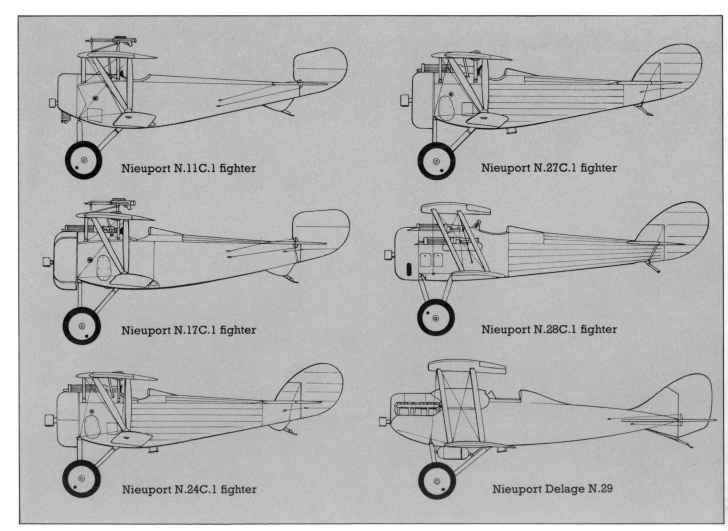

Nieuport N.11C.1 fighter

Nieuport N.27C.1 fighter

Nieuport N.17C.1 fighter

Nieuport N.28C.1 fighter

Nieuport N.24C.1 fighter

Nieuport Delage N.29

Above: A 1915 AEG G bomber, used in small numbers on operations over the Western Front.

impressive statistically, yet they had sown the seeds for similar and more effective formations in the following years.

On 25 May 1917 – merely weeks after the disbandment of 3 Wing RNAS– a loose formation of 21 Gotha bombers appeared over the southeastern corner of England and dropped a total of 159 bombs (5200 kgs) on random targets in Kent, killing 95 people and injuring a further 195. The raiders' only casualties were one Gotha destroyed in an explosion when attacked by Sopwith Pups of 4 Squadron RNAS, and a second which crashed in Belgium for no discernible reason – it was mooted that the pilot had a heart failure in midair. The Gothas' original target had been London, and only adverse winds had prevented them reaching the capital of the British Empire. Though isolated airplane raids had been flown against the United Kingdom almost from the outset of war, and airship raids had become frequent in 1916–17; this daylight raid by long-range heavy bombers created a near-panic among the British civil population. For the next 12 months German bombers continued to raid England, by day and by night, and were for the most part virtually unmolested by the British defenses. On 28 September 1917 the 25 Gothas which initially set out for England were accompanied by two *Riesenflugzeug* (Giant Airplanes) massive biplanes with wings spanning nearly 140 feet (almost the same span as the World War Two Boeing B-29 Superfortress). On this occasion weather conditions forced the majority to abort the mission, but the Gothas and the R-planes were to return again and again over the ensuing months, creating havoc and destruction. From May 1917 to May 1918 a total of 27 day and night raids were made against English targets by Gothas, while R-planes alone flew just 11 sorties. In all a total of 111,935 kgs of bombs was dropped, killing 835 and injuring 1972 people, causing an official total damage costing £1,418,272.

When compared with the appalling air-raid casualties caused by bombing in 1939–45, such figures may seem relatively trivial. To the civil population of the period, however, they created a mounting fury and an immediate public outcry for primitive retaliation in kind, a task utterly outside the capability of the existing Allied air services. No Allied aircraft in 1917–18 was able to carry a bomb load into the heart of Germany and return to base, though just prior to the Armistice of November 1918 three examples of the Handley Page V/1500 bomber were standing by in Norfolk, ostensibly for a first raid against the German capital, Berlin. The tangible effects of the uproar against the Gotha raids were, mainly, twofold. Primarily, it led to the formation of the 41st Wing, RFC in October 1917, composed initially of three bomber squadrons intended for strategic attacks on German industry. This in turn was absorbed into VIII Brigade in February 1918, which in turn was the nucleus of the Independent Force, RAF, created in May 1918 under the command of Hugh Trenchard. The latter force was solely tasked with strategic bombing of Germany. The second important outcome of the German airplane attacks was, ironically, the eventual formation of the Royal Air Force as a single service. A governmental inquiry into Britain's aerial defenses was headed by the South African veteran Jan Smuts, whose eventual report recommended in essence a complete reorganization and amalgamation of the RFC and RNAS into a separate (from Army and Navy control) air service, with its own ministry and annual budget. From this report came the formation of the Royal Air Force with effect from 1 April 1918.

By mid-1917 the unceasing striving by each country's aircraft designers for better war machines had begun to bear fruit. On the Allied fronts the Farnborough-designed SE5 scout had joined with the Sopwith Camel and Bristol F2b two-seat fighter in combatting the latest German Albatros scouts and the newly introduced Fokker Dr 1 triplanes, while the French fighter pilots were now flying Spad S7 scouts alongside the latest

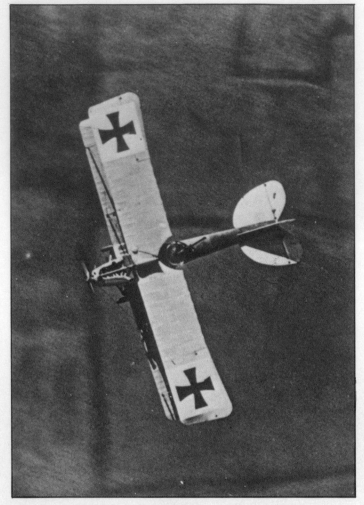

Above: **An Albatros C.III viewed over the Belgian Front. The rear observer and his defensive machine gun are well evidenced.**
Above right: **Death in the air – an Allied two-seater on its death plunge, one of the rare authentic photos of combat during 1914–18.**

Nieuport variants. In the reconnaissance field, the RE8 ('Harry Tate') had replaced the outdated BEs, and Germany had equipped many front-line units with improved Albatros, Rumpler, LVG and Halberstadt two-seaters. In April 1917 the USA joined the Allied struggle against Germany, though apart from such volunteer units as the *Escadrille Lafayette* serving with the French, American air crews were flying British and French airplanes in regular Allied units and would continue to do so until well into 1918 before the first all-American squadrons began operations in France. Even then no American-designed aircraft saw active service in Europe before the Armistice. The naval facets of the aerial war were catered for mainly by a bewildering variegation of flying boat and float-plane designs, a majority of these being used primarily for coastal-water patrols seeking submarines or enemy shipping.

The period 1917–18 saw the aerial fighting over the Western Front reach a peak of activity. It was a time of the legendary aces of aviation military history when the exploits of such men as Manfred von Richthofen, Werner Voss, 'Jimmy' McCudden, 'Mick' Mannock, 'Billy' Bishop, Georges Guynemer, Rene Fonck, Charles Nungesser and a host of other fighter pilots of equal prowess echoed throughout the media of the world. In this, the first aerial conflict in human history, such youngsters set the pattern for all future air combat. There was no textbook of rules to follow, no rigid tactics to apply. All such matters were

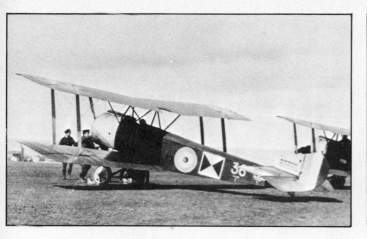

Above left: No. 3 Wing, RNAS was the first true strategic bombing unit formed by the Allies, in 1916. Part of its equipment were these Sopwith 1½ Strutter single-seat bombers, with N5107 in the foreground.
Above: Germany's development of strategic bombing was exemplified by the formation of the 'England Squadron' – *Kagohl Nr 3* – equipped with long-range Gotha bombers for attacks on English targets from Belgian bases in 1917.

empirical, learned and practiced by the only method available – sheer experience. If a tyro pilot managed to survive his first few sorties 'over the lines' – and a majority of casualties did occur to men flying their first operations – he stood a fair chance of surviving. Lessons were ingrained quickly when death awaited the unwary or slow-witted. In the arena of the unbounded skies such a death could arrive with a swiftness which baffled the mind; a moment's relaxation often meant oblivion from an unknown, unseen hand. Aircraft were imperfect, engines too often unreliable, and pilots – with rare exceptions – flew without even the consolation of a parachute should their machine be crippled or set afire. In the latter case – not uncommon a conclusion to any combat – many crews chose to abandon their aircraft rather than die in a holocaust of gasoline flames. Instances of traditional chivalry between fighting men were occasional exceptions to a form of life and death struggle where mercy was a rare emotion and the overriding urge was simply to kill, by any and every method opportunity offered. The commonest tactic was to fasten on an opponent's tail, then shoot him in the back.

If the fighter pilot found little glory in his daily task of seeking, fighting and killing, the lot of the unpublicized crews of the lumbering bomber or reconnaissance aircraft was doubly unglamorous. Flying a machine of inferior performance and maneuverability to any attacking enemy fighter, the two-seater pilots and observers could only rely on determination and sheer courage to survive. Aerial 'marking' or 'spotting' for the earthbound artillery – a prime function for such crews – meant flying on a predetermined course, at a relatively low altitude, above enemy troop dispositions for unending hours. They thus became easy prey for accurate antiaircraft fire from the ground, or any of the dashingly painted, roving fleet *jagd-*

Below: The largest British-designed bomber to see extensive operational use was the Handley Page 0/100 and its derivative 0/400. The first HP 0/100 (No. 3116) landed in France on 4 March 1917, seen here with its 100-foot wings overshadowing a Sopwith Triplane and Nieuport Scout.

staffeln or *escadrilles* of fighters. Lacking the speed to out-distance any such opposition, their sole salvation was a stout observer-gunner and the luck of the gods. Photoreconnaissance, an adjunct to infantry operations which grew rapidly in importance from the opening months of the war, called equally for stoic endurance under fire as clumsy glass plates were changed individually by hand until the job was accomplished. Such men were the unsung heroes of the aerial war, crews whose sacrifices and dogged devotion to their duties were seldom accorded their due in awards or even publicity. The same could be said of the night bombers. Venturing over enemy-occupied territory in the raven blackness of a night sky, attempting to navigate accurately with only the stars and a minimum of mechanical aids, and running a gauntlet of probing searchlights and ground gunfire; the 'minions of the moon' blazed a precarious path for future generations of night bombers.

In the nonoperational zones were the vast training establishments, human 'factories' and 'production lines' for the ever-hungry demands of the first-line squadrons, where an unending stream of pilots and observers were given ab initio instruction in their future crafts. Here too methods and means were to a degree empirical for the greater part of the war. Instructors were, more than often, merely ex-operational crews being 'rested' from wounds or active service generally. Such veterans were seldom truly qualified for the intrinsic needs of imparting their hard-won experience successfully to embryo airmen. Too many had yet to recover mentally from the ordeal of front-line aerial combat before being shuffled hastily into an instructor's role, and were thus psychologically unfit to carry out such duties with the complete dedication and full enthusiasm which always marks the born teacher. The aircraft in which they were expected to perform their duties hardly inspired confidence overall – machines which, in many cases, were underpowered, unreliable, or simply too 'long in the tooth.' With occasional exceptions, such as the De Havilland 6 or Avro 504J, few training aircraft had been originally *designed* as instructional machines and lacked even elementary training aids. The mortality rates among would-be pilots in all air services were high throughout the war – yet no air service was ever short of waiting volunteers eager to refill empty cockpits. Flying still retained the aura of the pioneers, an adventure into the unknown which, with the added pseudoglamour of a war-time overlay, gave aviation a charisma unresistable to the youth of the day.

By mid-1917, and particularly throughout 1918, the aerial war had resolved itself into recognizable divisions. The fighter squadrons now flew and fought as well-drilled teams,

Left: Nieuport 27 Scout of No. 1 Squadron, RFC at Bailleul on 27 December 1917, piloted by the Canadian ace, Captain Wendell Rogers.
Below left: Albatros D.II, D1724/16, the mount of the German ace Carl Schafer who was eventually killed in combat on 5 June 1917 and credited with 30 victories. The ply-covered fuselage, twin-gun armament, and graceful lines gave birth to many standard features in later fighter designs.
Right: Captain George Guynemer of *Escadrille* N3 in his Nieuport 23 Scout, with the Stork insignia, in 1916.
Below: Spad S VII, *Vieux Charles*, personal mount of the legendary French ace Georges Guynemer, seen here at Dunkirk, 1917. The fuselage insignia – a Stork – marked a tactical fighting force of ace units – the *Cigognes*.

coordinated and led by veteran aces; the day of the lone wolf, exemplified superbly in 1916 by Albert Ball, VC and Werner Voss, were clearly past. Perhaps the most obvious examples of this shift in tactical use were such 'groups' as the German *Jagdgeschwader Nr 1*, the so-termed 'Richthofen Circus,' which came into being on 26 June 1917 when four *jagdstaffeln* – Nos. 4, 6, 10 and 11 – became a self-contained 'flying squad' under the single, overall direction of Rittmeister Manfred von Richthofen. Its appellation 'Circus' by Allied crews was apt because the purpose of JG.1 was simply as a travelling entity to be added to any local air formations along the battle-front where air supremacy was necessary for vital ground operations. The nearest equivalent Allied group of units was the French combination of fighter *escadrilles* known as *Les Cigognes* (The Storks) which included in its ranks virtually every top-scoring pilot of 1916–18 at some period. Though each unit bore a Stork insigne on the fuselages of its Nieuports or Spads, it was, nevertheless, not a totally coordinated fighting formation in the same mold as the Richthofen Circus; it was rather a gathering of French elite aces who continued to fly individually. The RFC and RAF formed no such groups per se, although by 1918 combined attacks on enemy airfields et al by three or four squadrons within the same Wing or Brigade were not uncommon. In every air service, however, the 'squadron' (or its equivalent) remained the basic fighting *unit;* 15 to 24 fighter pilots led by a single commander who received overall direction from his higher echelons of authority, but who then decided specific tactics and other details on his own authority.

Most squadron commanders in all services were fighting leaders, participating in most of the day-to-day operations whenever other responsibilities permitted.

A large part of the 1918 fighters' responsibilities was escorting and protecting the two-seater photoreconnaissance and day-bomber squadrons. The prime purpose of all air services remained as support for land armies' operations, and despite the fulsome glamour attached to fighter exploits both during 1914–18 and indeed ever since, a fighter's *prime* function was to prevent enemy reconnaissance and ensure free passage for its own recce aircraft over enemy territory. Fighter-versus-fighter combat, though necessary and, in the eyes of the layman, enthralling, was nevertheless secondary to the chief duty of all fighter pilots – protection and spearhead for their comrades in the 'army cooperation' squadrons. Before the close of 1917, and increasingly in 1918, however, fighter pilots were often used as additional forward artillery when they undertook ground-strafing and low-level bombing of opposing infantry trenches, troops and installations. This was a form of warfare which meant running the gauntlet of murderous barrages of small-arms' fire at virtually zero height, and inevitably incurred high casualties.

Throughout 1918 the Allied air services fought the air war with aircraft first introduced to operations in early 1917 for the most part, but Germany continued its striving for superior designs and in April 1918 the first examples of a new fighter, the Fokker D VII, began to reach front-line *staffeln*. Within three months some 400 D VIIs were being flown at the battle-

Above: The most successful combat fighter in any air service throughout 1914–18, the Sopwith Camel first entered service in June 1917. This example, D9445, is being tested at Mousehold Heath Aerodrome, Norwich, England, prior to delivery to the RAF in 1918, where it served with Nos. 151 and 152 (Nightfighter) Squadrons.

Right: The Camel's closest rival as an ideal dogfighter was Germany's Fokker Dr1 triplane of 1917–18. This example, 404/17, was the personal steed of Hauptmann Adolf Ritter von Tutschek, seen here about to take off from Foulis in March 1918. He was killed on 15 March 1918.

Below: Contemporary with the Camel as a classic fighter was the Farnborough-designed SE5a scout of 1917. This example, D3511, camouflaged for an antiobservation balloon sortie, belonged to 40 Squadron RAF, whose commander, Australian Roderic Dallas, is pictured in its cockpit on 28 May 1918.

fronts, and its superior performance in all facets proved it to be the most successful German fighter in major use of the war. Before the November Armistice further fresh fighters had entered operational service, including the Fokker E V and the Siemens-Schuckert D III and D IV scouts. In the RAF squadrons the only new fighter to see reasonable war service that year was the Sopwith Snipe, successor and stablemate to the famous Sopwith Camel while the French and American units received such improved versions of well-established types as the Nieuport 28 Scout and the Spad 13. On the bomber scene came the De Havilland 9a, a reengined and redesigned variant of the earlier ill-starred DH9. Several DH9a units, including those of the US Marine Corps, flew the new type during the closing months of the war, and the 'Ninak' – as it was dubbed by its RAF crews – was to offer sterling service for a further decade in the postwar RAF. German two-seaters had also been much progressed by mid-1918, with designs like the Rumpler C VII being capable of operating at a ceiling of more than 23,000 feet. One German designer, Dr Hugo Junkers, had abandoned the contemporary fixation with fabric-skinned, wood box-framed construction, and introduced a number of monoplanes and biplanes of all-metal manufacture, including a corrugated 2-mm dural skin for all surfaces which was to be a Junkers' feature for many years to come.

With the signing of the Armistice, all war operations ceased

(officially) at 1100 hours on 11 November 1918. The immediate effect on the aviation scene was a near-complete halt in both production and progress in design. The German air services surrendered some 15,000 aircraft and 27,000 aero engines in accordance with the terms of the cease-fire treaty, while in Britain, France and the United States multithousands of aircraft contracted for manufacture were abruptly cancelled. The need for pure quantitative strength was now nullified; the RAF, for merely one example, possessed 3300 airplanes and 103 airships of all types at that date – the largest single air force in the world. It was the close of an era unique in human history, inasmuch as it had been the first-ever conflict between nations in which airplanes had figured as instruments of war. That generation of airmen had created an entirely new form of warfare, with no precedents from which to learn means and methods. Each lesson learned had been acquired at the personal risk of life and limb. The airplanes they flew gave only the barest protection from death or disaster; they were sturdy but strictly utilitarian, providing a bald minimum of physical comfort. All crews had flown in open cockpits, totally exposed to crippling cold at altitudes of up to 23,000 feet, lacking oxygen and heating, completely unprotected from the debilitating effects of decreasing air pressure. Yet the tradition they carved out was to be a base-rock foundation for all succeeding generations of men and machines.

Above: No American-designed aircraft saw operational service in World War I, but American designers produced a proliferation of ostensible 'warplanes'; just one example was this Sturtevant 'Battleplane' of 1918. The wing-mounted gun 'boxes' were an unconscious tribute to the courage of all 1914–18 aerial gunners!

Right: Fokker D VII, F 5125/18 in all-white finish, the personal aircraft of Oberleutnant Hermann Göring when he commanded *Jagdgeschwader Nr 1, Richthofen* in late 1918. Göring was later to recreate the German Luftwaffe and command it from 1935 until 1945.

Below: The unceasing striving by all countries' aircraft designers throughout 1915–18 toward better war machines resulted in a bewildering variety of shapes and ideas. The German firm Siemens-Schuckert's first single-seat fighter biplane was this SSW DD5 first tested in August 1916 but not accepted for production. Behind it is another of the firm's designs, the SSW E.1 monoplane fighter of 1916.

On Peaceful Wings

The world's first air passenger services – fare-paying and in relative luxury – were those provided by the German airship company *Deutsche Luftfahrts Aktien Gesellschaft* (DELAG) which, from 1910 to 1914, carried some 35,000 fare-paying passengers between various German cities in the company's Zeppelin rigid airships – and without a single fatality or even serious casualty among its customers. As a vehicle for such an enterprise, however, the contemporary airplanes were woefully inadequate in general, though an occasional exception afforded an inkling of just such a use in the future. One example of the latter was Claude Grahame-White's *Charabanc* of 1913 – a long-nacelled biplane in which he often took aloft up to 10 passengers for a 'joy-ride' from his Hendon airdrome. Incidentally, it was the aircraft from which a Mr W Newell made the first parachute drop in Great Britain on 9 May 1914; he was 'booted' from a precarious perch on the *Charabanc's* undercarriage at 2000 feet over Hendon and descended safely in the middle of that airfield minutes later.

The outbreak of war in August 1914 automatically stifled all further civil aviation for the duration of hostilities, though it might be noted that at least one British visionary, George Holt Thomas, displayed his faith in the future by registering Britain's first civil airline firm – the Aircraft Transport and Travel Ltd – in London on 5 October 1916. The immediate post-Armistice months of 1918–19 saw the Royal Air Force inaugurate a series of aerial mail and freight services between England and Germany, supplying the Allied Army of Occupation, but true civil aviation did not come into being until 1 May 1919. The first regular scheduled commercial passenger and freight services from Britain actually commenced on 25 August 1919. In the same year parallel national airlines were inaugurated by Belgium, France and the United States, the latter's first inter-

To a modern generation of travellers, well used to an almost mundane experience of being smoothly transported by day or by night to almost any destination desired around the globe by air, in comfort, safety, and on planned-to-the-minute schedules; the myriad problems – and their solutions – facing the pioneering air lines and their crews may now seem not only 'ancient history' but even semicomical. Any such complacency with Concorde-type facilities now commonly available merely emphasizes the present-day unconscious acceptance of air travel as a normal mode of transportation of freight, mail or passengers, as familiar as the automobile or diesel train. Yet it is little more than a man's biblical allotment of 'three score years and ten' since aerial transportation first became a reality.

Above: Beyond removal of its war equipment, this De Havilland 9 of the Aircraft Transport and Travel Ltd Company offered the barest luxury to would-be passengers, whose voluminous flying garments were necessary to combat the exposure to roaring slipstream and icy temperatures on route.

Below: Early attempts to produce passenger-carrying aircraft often involved drastically modified variants of standard wartime machines. This Bristol Type 28 three-seat 'Tourer' was an obvious spin-off of the Bristol F2b Fighter of 1917, and was exhibited in this form at the 1919 Olympia. The power was from a 230 hp Siddeley Puma engine.

national scheduled passenger service beginning on 1 November 1919 by the Aeromarine West Indies Airways between Key West, Florida, and Havana, Cuba. The aircraft used in all cases were crude conversions of aircraft designed originally – mainly – as bombers, and the dubious 'privilege' of becoming a fare-paying occupant of the cramped, plywood or fabric-covered cockpits available offered little in the way of compensating comfort en route. Heating comprised a swaddling of fur-lined coats, scarves and thick gloves to combat a rushing, icy slipstream, while en route refreshments depended entirely on self-provision by the customer. Even eventual arrival at any stated destination could not be guaranteed, let alone at a

specified hour – shades of 1980 airlines! – and success or otherwise remained very dependent on the vagaries of European weather conditions.

The earliest consideration given to passengers took the form of locally produced cabin structures built around what had originally been the rear gunners' cockpits, or, in the case of 'heavy' aircraft such as the Handley Page 0/400 conversions, an internal lounge, highly decorated and incorporating wicker cane seating (for weight lightness) and square windows cut in the fuselage sides for outward observation. Heating remained virtually nonexistent, and the noise and vibration from the engines were unabated throughout the journey. Despite these discomforts and vicissitudes, it should be borne in mind that – apart from wartime fliers – few civilians 'had ever taken to the air in the immediate postwar years; flying in any shape or form was still akin to an adventure for the layman, almost a pioneering experience with all the associated excitement and novelty of such affairs. Inherited from the vast expansion of the flying services during the war was a host of reasonably well-equipped airfields. It was one of these – the old RFC/RAF training airdrome at Hounslow, now part of the site of London's Heathrow airport – which became England's first commercial airdrome for regular airline traffic. On 29 March 1920 Hounslow's facilities for Customs clearance et al were effectively transferred to Croydon (or Waddon, as the airport was then titled), and the latter was officially opened for scheduled airlines the following year on 31 March. It was to remain London's premier airport for the next two decades.

For those first few years of the peace prospective airline passengers in most countries had a varied selection of airlines from which to choose, most of which were logical off-shoots of established aircraft manufacturers. Examples in Britain included Handley Page Transport, Instone Air Lines and the British Marine Air Navigation Company. On 1 April 1924, however, most such private ventures were incorporated in the government-sponsored national airway titled Imperial Airways. This new airline lost little time in opening fresh scheduled intercity routes around Europe, though it should be remembered that many such routes had already been well established by its predecessor independent companies. Subsidized by the British government, and with widespread preassistance in survey flights by the overseas sections of the Royal Air Force, Imperial Airways looked beyond Europe and commenced surveyance of future routes to India, South Africa and Australia. Many of these were led by Alan Cobham who was later knighted for his many pioneering services to civil aviation.

The prime goal was to open the airways to India, and in April 1929 Imperial Airways commenced operations on various trans-Mediterranean services as a vital first stage toward

Above: In Britain a host of private flying clubs and commercial firms mushroomed in the 1920s, and one mainstay design flown was the ubiquitous Avro 504K two-seater.
Right: Though the first official carriage of mail by air in the United States occurred as early as September 1911, the 'golden years' of American airmail pilots came post-1918, utilizing mainly modified DH4 two-seaters and similar designs. Many of these men – one was a certain Charles Lindbergh – later helped pioneer American commercial aviation; one such pilot was Leon Cuddeback, seen here with his 'Swallow' biplane at Boise, Idaho, in 1926. Note his *de rigeur* dress of 'flight jacket,' breeches and riding boots.
Below right: Enclosed comfort soon became a priority with the early airlines – at least, for the passengers. This Vickers Vulcan, an eight-passenger design introduced initially in 1922, had a single 450-hp Napier Lion engine, and the pilot sat in an open cockpit just forward of the top wing center-section. This specific Vulcan, G-EBLB, was finally wrecked in July 1928 near Croydon Airport, England.

future Far East flights. In the previous month the airline had officially opened its London-to-Karachi commercial air route, but this was necessarily by stages only, and one leg had to be by train from Basle to Genoa due to disagreement with Italian authorities who refused air access above Italian territory then. The first regular commercial passenger line from London to Cape Town was inaugurated on 27 April 1932 – a scheduled journey taking 11 days – but it was to be a further three years before any similar facility became available for passengers wishing to fly to Australia. This latter route commenced in April 1935, took 12 and a half days for its overall 12,754-mile journey, and cost the customer £195 for a single, one-way fare. While such 'prestige' major routes attracted a deal of publicity, behind the headlines an increasingly interwoven pattern of internal aerial services and pathways were achieving regularity and high reliability, particularly in the contexts of mail and air freight; an ever-expanding spider's web of communication which provided businessmen, politician and layman alike with fresh opportunities for efficiency and fortune. Until the 1930s such enterprise was relatively unencumbered by officialdom – the air was virtually a free zone to be used as and when crews desired to fly – but the heavy hand of bureaucracy soon began to be manifested after 1930 by an increasing mini-avalanche of rules, regulations, restrictions and omni-present paperwork to be completed and authorized prior to permission being granted for any flight over British territory. The hitherto freedom of transit of the skies was rapidly curtailed, regulated and patterned into the tight parameters of governmental control – usually under the label of safety but too often merely as an extension of Civil Service autocracy.

Above: The Curtiss Condor of 1934 – twin 700 hp Wright Cyclone radial engines – is usually regarded as the last American biplane airliner in regular services, and, incidentally, is claimed to be the first 'sleeper' airliner in the world.

Right: Handley Page W.10, G-EBMR, *City of Pretoria*, which entered Imperial Airways in March 1926 is seen here at Croydon Airport. Note the still-open cockpit for pilots.

Below: Passenger accommodation in one of six Handley Page 0/7 aircraft – conversions of the wartime 0/400 bomber – ordered by the Chinese Government in 1919.

The relatively rapid adjustment of aviation from its wartime employment as an agent of destruction to placid use for transportation and global communication proceeded on roughly parallel lines in all nations, varying only by the limits of each nation's resources. Over the vast stretches of the United States prospective airlines were faced with internal flight distances far greater than any European equivalent, apart from vast differences in temperatures and weather conditions between certain states. Much of America's early pioneering flying aimed to extend and improve internal communications, especially in the context of the postal services. The saga of the early airmail pilots and crews deserve a thick volume to record their deeds as the latest inheritors of the legendary Pony Express horsemen of yesteryear. Their steeds were open cockpit, war-designed DH4 two-seaters, Curtiss JN4 'Jennies,' and other sturdy biplanes – vehicles hardly ideal for battling through rain, wind or snow blizzards, over mountain and desert, across poorly charted wastes, and maintained under primitive conditions en route at airfields which might better be described as landing strips and offered only the barest technical resources. Nevertheless, the flying mailmen persevered. The first *regular* airmail service anywhere in the United States was started in August 1918 between New York City and Washington, DC, while the initial coast-to-coast mail service by air was flown from San Francisco to Long Island, New York,

on 22/23 February 1921. Within three years regular east-west and west-east airmail services were in operation. By its very nature such postal services were by set stages – a total of 14 in the coast-to-coast context – but their greatest virtues were regularity and dependability. To maintain these standards the airmail crews flew in all weathers, by day and by night, winter and summer, despite an alarming casualty rate in aircraft and crews. Such men epitomized the old spirit of the US Postal Service motto – 'The mail *must* go through.'

While those doughty mailmen battled through storms and other facets of raw nature to fulfill their appointed task, embryo airlines were taking their first faltering steps. In a nation dedicated to the ideal of private enterprise and overt individual achievement, the new commercial enterprise offered wide opportunities and – to the more visionary – a bright future. Three basic ingredients were vital for airliners – safety, speed and passenger comfort – if such commercial ventures were to become attractive to customers. Add to these reliability of announced schedules, a factor which quickly assumed equal priority and which led inadvertently to a number of unnecessary accidents and fatalities during the proving years of American civil aviation. Improvement in customer comfort was an objective easily obtained, but reliability – and thereby safety – depended to a major degree on powerful enough engines of proven stamina and output under the myriad

operating circumstances of the period. Development of the airline industry in the United States was surprisingly slow in the 1920s. Governmental subsidies were aimed almost wholly at the airmail services, leaving the host of individually financed companies to provide their own financial backing and, inevitably, to take all risks upon themselves. In 1927, however, the US Government released its bureaucratic grip on air mail, opening the field to private competition. By the 1930s American airlines – by then mainly merged conglomerates of many of the initial, small private firms – finally began to become viable commercially.

In Europe in the 1920s France, Belgium and Holland tended to dominate the internal routes, with the British airlines overlapping the network. Germany, crushed under the terms of the Versailles Treaty, had been specifically forbidden any form of military air service; yet, surprisingly, official permission was granted on 8 January 1919 to the *Deutsche Luftreederei GmbH* firm to operate an airline. The first regular airlines within postwar Germany began operations that same month, to be followed by several other internal airlines. The German aircraft industry, now without its massive wartime impetus, attempted to produce civil transports from crude conversions of wartime designs, but all their efforts to revitalize German aviation were abruptly stifled after June 1919 when Germany signed the Versailles Treaty. The latter's harsh punitive terms not only expressly forbade all military aviation, including manufacture, but even denied the import of foreign aircraft. Civil aviation ground to a standstill. For the next three years all attempts to inaugurate any form of airline were to be nullified by overzealous Allied authorities. It was not until 1 February 1922 that the Allies relented and permitted construction of civil aircraft in Germany, commencing in May. They specified, among other restrictive stipulations, that no single-seat design was allowed to have more than 60-hp power, weight must not exceed 600 kilos, maximum ceiling was to be 4000 meters, and maximum speed under full power was not to exceed 170 km per hour at 2000 meters. On 1 January 1923 Germany regained control of its skies when, in accordance with Clause 320 of the treaty, Allied aircraft ceased to own an exclusive right to land in or fly over Germany at will.

Against a backcloth of roaring inflation, massive unemployment and widespread dissention and unrest, a number of newly registered aircraft firms began producing light sporting designs. In deep secrecy the German Defense Ministry ordered construction of 100 Fokker D XIII fighters and some Heinkel He-1s for the German Navy – all to be assembled and tested outside German territory, then 'imported' in crates for ostensible resale to an unidentified South American country. Sales of any aircraft within Germany were virtually impossible under the glowering clouds of impending financial collapse of the economy, and such manufacturers as Junkers, Dornier, Udet and Heinkel set up markets abroad, particularly in South American countries. By the mid-1920s, however, German aviation had blossomed steadily in the pure sporting field, with a host of exhibitions, displays and annual race meetings. All were very well attended by an increasingly aviation-minded

Right: With a two-man crew and relatively luxurious accommodation for 20 passengers, the Armstrong Whitworth Argosy airliner began its commercial service in 1926. In the following year customers were being offered 'luxury' lunches and a buffet bar facility between Croydon and Paris, at a one-way fare of £4. G-EBOZ, titled *City of Arundel*, is seen here at Khartoum after completing the Cairo-Khartoum sector of an inaugural England-to-Central Africa route in March 1931. *Below:* As commercial aviation burgeoned globally in the late 1920s, the flying boat became a serious contender for the long-distance routes. The Short brothers' *Calcutta* emerged as a development of the Singapore I in early 1928, and entered service with Imperial Airways. One example, F-AJDB, was built specifically to a French government order and first flew in September 1929. Fitted out for 15 passengers, the *Calcutta* enhanced luxury standards internally, though its two-pilot cockpit was open in the nose.

civil population. Top aerobatic pilots like the wartime fighter aces Ernst Udet, von Greim, Paul Baumer and Gerhard Fieseler became national heroes as they consistently thrilled hundreds of thousands of spectators with consummate skill and daring in the sky. Their mounts were light-powered biplanes, capable of degrees of tight maneuverability impossible to match in any monoplane, providing the onlooker with breathtaking spectacles of the true 'art' of pilotmanship.

On 6 January 1926 the German civil airline Lufthansa officially came into being, and on the following 16 June the Allied authorities brought an end to the cramping restrictions on construction of aircraft in Germany. The way was now clear for rapid progress in home-grown civil aviation. By then, nevertheless, many designers' future projects were proceeding with an eye on possible contracts for the clandestine military air service already being formed. Thus several designs for the larger civil airliners could, with modest modification, be simply converted ultimately to become troop transporters or bombers. Toward this goal the main trend in fresh aircraft was in monoplane configuration; the era of the beloved biplane in Germany was already on the wane, as the aircraft industry became widely involved in preparing for the future Luftwaffe as the most modern air force in the world. At the head of the recently created Lufthansa was Erhard Milch, an ex-wartime observer whose ruthless drive and self-centered ambitions were eventually to take him to a peak of power in the World War II Luftwaffe. Perhaps indicative of Milch's vision for the future of German aviation was the first four-engined airliner to be accepted for Lufthansa use, the Udet U-11 *Kondor* – a high-wing monoplane.

Left: Unquestionably the 'Queens' of all Imperial Airways' biplane airliners were the Handley Page 42 'gentle giants,' introduced on European and, later, overseas routes from 1931. Elegant in accommodation and stately in performance, the 'Flying Bananas' – a nickname derived from the design's extra-long slim fuselage – continued in service until 1940. In this view of Croydon Airport are (foreground) HP *Heracles* (G-AAXC) and *Horatius* (G-AAXD). Cruising speed was a leisurely 100 mph, and wings spanned 130 feet.
Below: Night Flight: the HP 42 *Horatius* alongside Croydon's air-traffic control tower.

If the rejuvenation of civil aviation in Germany was clearly linked with adoption of the monoplane for its growing international airline network, Britain's Imperial Airways continued to rely heavily on the trusted, lumbering biplane until well into the 1930s. Chief among the designs to enter service during that period were such sedate giants as the De Havilland 66 *Hercules*, Armstrong Whitworth *Argosy*, and, in the early 1930s, the Handley Page *Hannibal*, while many of the Empire routes were flown by such biplane flying boats as the Short *Calcutta* and *Scipio*. Each provided a level of passenger comfort and service considered semiluxurious for those years, while reliability reached high peaks in the contexts of scheduled timings and, by no means least, safety. The one aspect of communication travel the biplane failed to provide, however, was speed. The first example of the HP *Hannibal* type of airliner to be delivered to Imperial Airways – in June 1931 – could carry up to 24 passengers and freight, but had a maximum speed of barely 120 mph. Nevertheless, the standards of customer comfort, particularly cuisine – including four- to seven-course meals en route – outweighed any dubious advantages of mere speed in transit. *Hannibal* and her stablemate H-class airliners gave faithful service for nearly 10 years on both European and Empire routes, accumulating an enviable record of some 2.3 million miles flown without a single passenger fatality. Indeed, in July 1937 one of those gentle mammoths, the HP *Heracles*, became the first commercial aircraft in the world to complete one million flown miles in passenger service. And in the present-day era of multimillion-pound costs for any supersonic airliner, it might be remembered that the average cost of an HP *Hannibal* in the 1930s was a mere £21,000.

Despite Britain's sloth in entering the monoplane age of aerial transport, by the mid 1930s the bulk of the world's airlines was equipped with the sleeker, faster single-winged airplane; leaving the doughty biplane to continue its long contribution to purely internal routes and services and as the backbone of the myriad private flying clubs and organizations. The metal clad monoplane airliner ushered in what amounted to a fresh era of air travel, providing a regularity and almost mundane form of aerial transition which rapidly came to be accepted by the travelling public as normal. The true pioneering days were long past; civil aviation had now become 'respectable.'

Clown and Circus

The miracle of man-flight, particularly during aviation's first three decades, provided a thrilling spectacle of unprecedented proportion to the average citizen, and every opportunity to actually witness an airplane flying was usually attended by a multitude of eager spectators. The earliest pilots were regarded as a race apart – 'intrepid birdmen' whose audacious feats brought them international fame, though seldom fortune. By 1910, a mere seven years since the Wright brothers had demonstrated man's mastery of the air, a number of those pioneering pilots had become household names in each country, feted and lauded wherever they flew. One such pilot was the Englishman, Claude Grahame-White who learned to fly in France, then returned to England, cleared some 200 acres of pastureland at Hendon, north of London, and made it his base for a succession of exhibitions and his private school for pilot tuition. A born showman, 'G-W' probably did more to make the British population air-minded than any other individual in the pre-1914 years. In the fashion of the period, he participated in various prize air races, staged flying displays at Hendon – by 1912, the Mecca for all aviation enthusiasts – and also pursued a personal campaign to impress the importance and potential of aviation upon government and public alike.

Grahame-White was but one of a host of international pilots who thrilled the public with their daring and skill during the years preceding the disastrous war of 1914–18. Aviation knew few restrictions then and freedom of the air was literally applied to all airmen. National parochialism was also absent; the relatively small community of pioneer pilots came from all countries to compete in races and exhibitions, and intermingled with no rivalry other than the healthy spirit of competition and sheer enthusiasm for aeronautics. Briton, Frenchman and German mixed socially, rubbing shoulders as equal adventurers in this new form of human endeavor. The aircraft they flew were frail in structure, woefully underpowered in too many instances, and the mysteries of stresses and other significant aspects of aerodynamics were 'unknown country' in which designers and pilots alike were still stumbling with little precedent to guide them onto the path of safety and reliability. Such ignorance of the now well-established rules of aeronautics in no way deterred men – and women – from taking to the air at every opportunity. A carefree air pervaded the whole aviation scene of the day, and the sheer joy, even rapture, of flying felt by all airmen more than outweighed the more obvious risks to life, limb or vehicle. Deaths due to poor pilotage, fractious engines or plain structural failure were relatively frequent, yet such tragedies were never permitted to blight the general progress of flying. A near-

Right: **The age of commercialism in aviation began early, and one of the earliest registered companies was the Frank Hucks Waterplane Company in Britain. The firm's Henry Farman seaplane is seen here taxiing out from the beach of a Devonshire resort, pre-1914.**
Below: **Grahame-White's 1913 *Charabanc*, which set new world records for passenger carrying and weight endurance that year, is seen here with 'G-W' at the controls.**

54

Below: Claude Grahame-White, the epitome of the pre-1914 check-capped pioneers of aviation.
Bottom: Air-race meetings quickly became popular in every country, with Hendon and Brooklands becoming the main venues in Britain. Here Claude Grahame-White rounds the No. 2 pylon at Hendon in 1913 in the Farman which he used later for his famous 'Wake up England' campaign. The whole machine was painted a 'vivid blue' (sic).

tradition grew apace that became epitomized among the fighting squadrons during 1914–18: 'No mourning' for the dead – carry on flying. Nonfatal accidents were merely regarded as part and parcel of the everyday routine – provided the pilot walked away from the crash, it was considered to be simply an unfortunate landing.

Pure aerobatics as we know them in the present day had no place in the pre-1914 scene; aircraft were precarious enough without indulging in unnecessary straining of the structure. In any case, few pilots had any real grasp of the essentials of aeronautics in any technical context to be capable of judging precise limitations in maneuver or performance, a vital pre-requisite to true aerobatic flight. It was not a case that the early pilots failed to exploit the maneuverability of their fragile craft. From the first international air meet of 1909 at Rheims, and especially during the 1912–14 years, airplanes were flown almost with gay abandon as pilots strived to attain leading places in speed and endurance contests. The courage needed to undertake such perilous flying may be judged by the virtual dearth of protective gear available to pilots; at best, a leather lap-strap to 'secure' him to his wood-slat 'seat,' and, perhaps, one of the various commercial flying 'crash-helmets' for his head. Flying clothing was distinctly 'nonstandard'; thick woollen scarves and gloves added to a thick tweed jacket, with cloth-tied puttees around the ankles – all worn merely to combat the icy winds. From this eager host of dedicated pioneers emerged many notable pilots: Colonel Cody, Gustav Hamel, the Honorable C S Rolls – all destined to die in the air by 1914; 'Tom' Sopwith and Geoffrey de Havilland – both later to create international aircraft firms; Howard Pixton, B C Hucks, and Mrs Hilda Hewlett – the latter even teaching her naval officer son to fly; 'Will' Rhodes-Moorhouse, wealthy playboy who was destined to die in 1915 after 'earning' the first Victoria Cross ever awarded to a British airman; the Frenchmen Louis Noel and his compatriot Lieutenant 'Beaumont' (Conneau); Harry Hawker whose name was to grace the great manufacturing firm of post-1918 years; Hubert Latham, Bertram Dickson, whose vision of future aerial warfare fell on deaf ears in the governmental hierarchy of the day, and who died flying. These and a hundred others helped create the rules of the air for all succeeding generations of aviators to embellish.

Those pilots who indulged in trick-flying, as the term was then, moved the technical editor of the weekly magazine *Flight* to observe in 1913: 'Several accidents have resulted from the deliberate performance of tricks in the air, such as were at one time notorious in America, where several pilots have been killed in front of the spectators. Catering to the sensations of the crowd, these men display the most amazing nerve in making steep dives followed by banked turns in which the wings would approach to a vertical position. . . .' The stern reference to American notoriety in trick-flying alluded in part to the various flying exhibitions inaugurated in the United States from as early as 1910, when pilots like C F Willard, Glenn Curtiss, Charles Hamilton and Lincoln Beachey gave their public audiences thrilling displays with, apparently, little regard for safety. As in every other country, those American pioneer exhibition pilots often paid the ultimate penalty for their flirting with death. Many of the stunts which later generations of exhibition pilots were to undertake as standard – flying under bridges, retrieving handkerchiefs from the ground with a wing-tip, and so on – were first demonstrated in the pre-1914 era.

Below: Though many individual women had helped pioneer aviation, certain facets were still regarded as wholly masculine pursuits in 1919. That year, however, a Miss Sylvia Borden (left) jumped by Guardian Angel parachute from a Handley Page 0/400 at 1000 feet over Cricklewood Aerodrome, north London, creating a sensation.
Below left: A Sopwith Camel demonstrates its fluid maneuverability over a peaceful English landscape, 1918.

The start of the European war in 1914 automatically called a halt to all civil aviation in the participating nations, but the urge to 'stunt' in airplanes was now gradually channelled into perfecting mastery of the airplane for military purposes at the various Service instruction schools. By 1916 the need for training pilots in the art of fighting in the air had been fully appreciated, as each air service inaugurated the formation of single-seat fighter formations for front-line duties. Spinning, looping, banking tightly, rolling off the top of a semiloop and thereby reversing flight direction quickly – the so-termed 'Immelmann' maneuver; all these and other aspects of quick-maneuvering became recognized as vital for the embryo fighter pilot. If he was to survive the acid test of combat, the fighter pilot had to be able to fly almost by instinct; air fighting took place at speeds calculated to baffle normal reasoning. Only if a pilot was at one with his Pup, Camel, Fokker or Nieuport was he likely to see another sunrise. By 1918 all aviation services had formed special schools for training fighters, but one man for whom such specialization training was insufficient set out to apply the principle to all forms of flight – Robert Smith-Barry. At Gosport, near Portsmouth, Smith-Barry created a school for advanced flying, taking normally qualified pilots and proceeding to give them almost a free hand in testing both their aircraft and themselves for perfection in the art of pure flying. His overriding concern was to eliminate any fear of flying, to demonstrate that – properly treated – any airplane was a well-mannered, perfectly safe vehicle, which would respond beautifully to correct control under *any* circumstances. The men who went to Gosport – even veteran combat pilots –

quickly realized the difference between their own crude ab initio instruction and the satisfaction of properly applied pilotmanship. They were given free rein, even encouraged, to fly in every conceivable attitude, at high or ultralow heights; in a word, they were to become master of their craft. From this school was to come the RAF's Central Flying School creed of perfection, and Smith-Barry became known as the man who taught the world to *fly*.

Of all the many and varied aircraft designs produced in those war years, the pugnacious Sopwith F1 Camel probably came closest to being the ideal aerobatic fighting airplane. With its stubby rotary-engined nose and centrally located masses, the Camel displayed an ability to turn left or right with breathtaking rapidity – in the contemporary vernacular, it could turn on a sixpence – while its lightning response to the lightest of control movement gave pilots the impression that the Camel could read their thoughts and therefore was completely in harmony with their wishes. The Camel's fighting record from its introduction to combat service in June 1917

until the Armistice in November 1918 speaks volumes for its character – nearly 3000 claimed victories for its myriad pilots, more than any other individual fighter in any air force of the war. Among those Camel 'kings' emerged a handful of individuals whose pure handling of a Camel marked them as legends in their own time: 'Sam' Kinkead, Oliver Stewart, W G Moore and a South African named D V Armstrong. The latter's ability to 'wring out' a Camel left indelible impressions on those who were privileged to watch any of his demonstrations. One such spectator wrote:

. . . there comes the growing roar of a Rhone (*engine*) . . . it is a Camel coming fast and low towards the hangars. The machine approaches the tarmac, flying parallel with the hangars, and suddenly with a rapidity that makes one blink it flicks over in a roll. . . . That evolution was done at no more than fifteen feet from the ground. We caught a glimpse of the greasy belly of the Camel's fuselage, saw the wing tips miss the ground by a matter of twelve inches, gaped as the little kite swung round the right way up again, and, as one man, we let out a blasphemous ejaculation as we watched it sweep up and away in a steep climbing turn.

'The hum of the engine ebbed and flowed as the pilot ground-strafed the fields around the aerodrome. And then he came by again. The sun glinted on the spinning disc of his propeller as he roared towards us; we could hear the wail of Rafwires as the Camel gathered speed. A rabbit ran in terror as the low-flying plane whipped the grass into fluttering agitation. And then again – that flick roll. So for a quarter of an hour that Camel held our attention. Three times the pilot pulled a loop so low that, as he swept inverted above our heads, we could see for a

Left: Another common stunt was transference from or to a speeding automobile or airplane.
Below left: The crazy antics of the first postwar barnstormers are exemplified here by Harry 'Tex' McLaughlin, an American, hanging by his teeth from a trapeze under a 'Canuck' variant of the Curtiss JN4 in 1920. He was fatally injured on 20 September 1921 at the New York State Fair, Syracuse, in front of 50,000 spectators.
Below: Parachutes only became standard issue in the RAF after 1925, and early training experience was commonly practiced from special wing platforms on bombers, as on this Vickers Vimy at RAF Halton.

few fleeting moments intimate details within the cockpit – the instruments gleaming in the sun, the green canvas belt, the wings on the fellow's tunic, black, sleek hair and a hand gripping the stick. Meanwhile the Rhone was running at full bore, its note falling and rising, falling and rising, as the machine climbed and dived three times. And then he slipped away, leaving a faint smoke trail while we stood and watched, shook our heads and laughed. . . .'

D'Urban Victor Armstrong, DFC, was killed stunting a Camel on 13 November 1918, while serving with 151 (nightfighter) Squadron in France.

Let Major W G Moore, OBE, DSC, sum up most combat pilots' view of the Camel:

'The Camel, being totally unstable in all directions and very sensitive fore and aft, and much influenced by engine torque, was a death-trap for an inexperienced pilot. A skilled pilot could not wish for a better mount. To him it was like having a pair of wings strapped onto his shoulder blades. Once you knew them, you could do anything you liked with them and turn their peculiarities to advantage. They were wonderful in a dogfight because they could make the quickest change of direction of any machine that flew in that war. Its peculiarities made it the most manoeuvrable fighter ever built and the best all-round performer.'

The end of the war in Europe left each nation holding enormous stocks of wartime-built and designed aircraft which were no longer needed. Every military air force was rapidly reduced to a mere skeleton of its wartime peak strength, and the vast surplus of aircraft put up for public sale in some form. Some of

the initial purchasers were various aircraft manufacturing firms who then hopefully inaugurated commercial ventures in the freight and passenger-carrying 'airlines' of the day. A surprisingly large number of aircraft, however, were bought by individual pilots, mainly ex-wartime trained men, for personal use. And among these were many men who set out to make a living from pure exhibition flying for the public – the first true 'barn-stormers.' It was the beginning of the 'five-shilling flip,' the 'air circus,' and – for many thousands of ordinary citizens – an opportunity to have their first taste of the wonder of flight. The true aircraft 'spines' of the barnstorming fraternity during the 1920s and early 1930s were the Canadian Curtiss JN4 'Jenny' and the British Avro 504 in America and Britain respectively. Both designs had already given sterling service as trainers for each country's air forces during the war years, and were now to achieve far wider fame in an astonishing variety of aerial roles.

The wholly freelance nature of the first barnstormers in America attracted the gamut of existing pilots, from seasoned

Right: **The 'circus' atmosphere of the early air meetings often produced highly imaginative modifications to otherwise harmless aircraft. This upside-down 'bus' was a BE2c, G-EAHS, also known as the 'Jazz Bus,' in 1919.**
Below: **This 'parasol' monstrosity had started life as a Bristol F2b Fighter.**

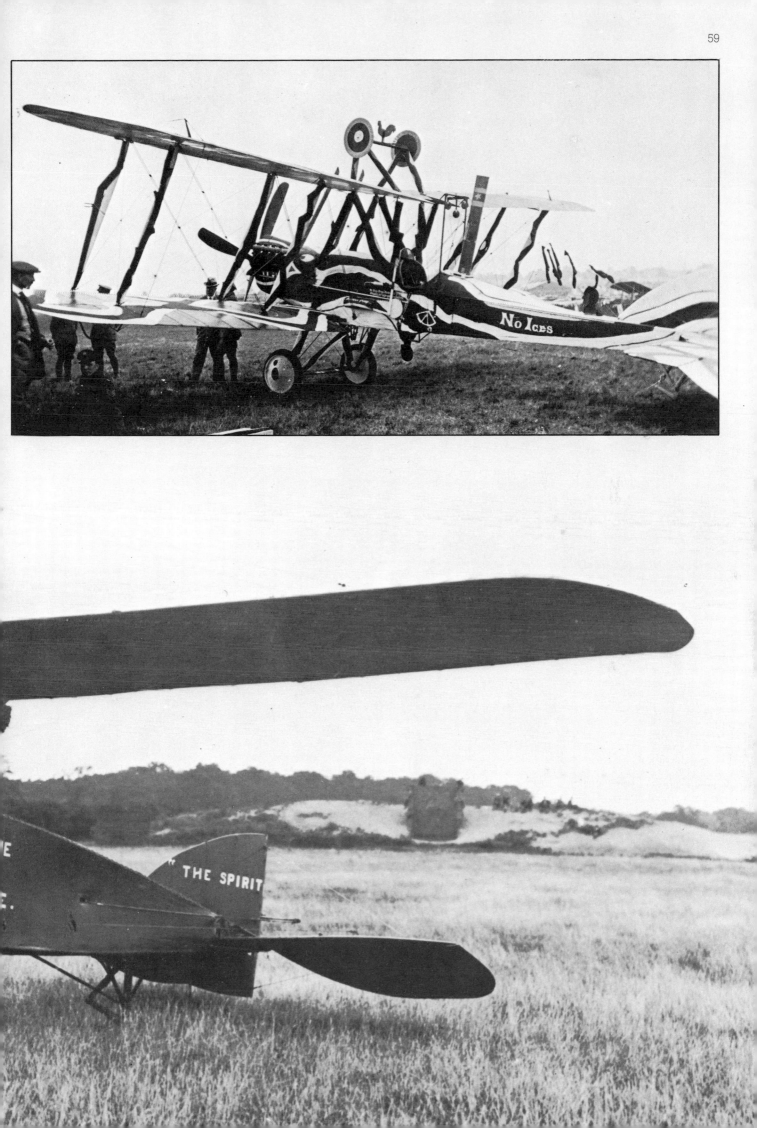

veterans to youngsters barely capable of taking off safely. The craze spread across every state, '. . . like a galloping disease,' as one contemporary critic phrased it, with a rash of highly dubious aircraft. They were barely maintained under literal in-the-field conditions – driven by pilots who ranged from serious, skilled practitioners of the 'art' to inexperienced striplings who – in a few cases – were learning to fly themselves as they offered potential passengers brief 'flips' for as little as $3.00 for 15 minutes 'aviating.' Inevitably, perhaps, the 'sport' also attracted a frantic fringe of certain individuals whose obsession with exhibitionism, egotism or plain bravado led them to perform tricks and stunts which, literally, took their life in their hands. Wing-walking, hanging from undercarriages, transferring by rope ladder from aircraft to motor car, or vice-versa, at speed, 'racing' against automobiles and speed boats, reproducing close-in 'dogfighting' à la 1918 warfare – these and a hundred other 'death-defying' exploits which catered to the morbid instincts of their spectators below. The barn-storming pilot was often dressed in what was almost uniform of the sport: leather top jerkin, riding corduroys, riding boots, leather helmet, and a long, flapping colored silk scarf trailing from the neck. It was a shoestring existence, hopping from state fair to state fair, exhibition, or local gathering; sleeping under the wings of the 'Jenny' when funds ran low; scrounging fuel and spares, and living the life of an aerial tramp.

In Britain similar venturers took to the air, selling 15-minute 'flips' for as little as 10 shillings (50p) – little more than one take-off, full circuit, and landing – though generally at a more sedate level than their US counterparts. No few rented their aircraft out to hirers for private or business flights – the forerunners of the air-taxi industry soon to come into general use. In Germany, despite heavy restrictions on all facets of aeronautics, many wartime pilots, such as Ernst Udet, Gerhard Fieseler, Paul Bäumer, Ritter von Schleich and others – coincidentally,

Previous page: Four Pitts S2A Specials of the Rothman's-sponsored civilian aerobatic team of the 1970s.
Above: The notorious *Pou du Ciel*, brainchild of the Frenchman Mignet, started a craze for homemade kit airplanes in the 1930s. This example, with pseudoregistration G-AFFI, was actually constructed in 1973–75 at Yeadon, and is now with the Nostell Aviation Museum.
Right: Martin Hearn on top of a Cornwall Aviation Company Avro 504 literally takes his life in his hands at an air display at Plymouth, Devon, on 21 August 1932.
Below: One of Jack Savage's Hendon fleet of skywriting SE5as, called 'The Sweep.'

mainly ex-fighter aces – pursued pure sporting exhibitions for a highly appreciative German public, attracting crowds of half a million spectators on occasion. The program of flying at such public displays varied little – in any country – but to a war-weary public seeking entertainment and momentary relief from an existence of increasing inflation, unemployment and mounting prices in everyday necessities, such pilots became national heroes in an otherwise depressing world. The expanding cinematic business opened other avenues for enterprising pilots. Stunt pilots, particularly, were in steady employment, as stand-ins for the movie stars in hair-raising feats of aerobatic flying, crashes and other facets of flying. Yet another field of activity was the commercial publicity business. Towing banners advertising domestic products or announcing forthcoming exhibitions and the like – all were grist to the barnstormer's mill.

One aspect of the showman pilot's repertoire which is still very much in evidence today was skywriting and smoke patterns. Credit for the invention of skywriting is usually accorded to Major J C Savage in Britain, who gathered together a band of ex-wartime pilots and some SE5as and taught them his specialized techniques for using the sky as a blackboard. His scheme was aimed almost entirely at the advertising business, though he personally continued experimentation and, from May 1924, began to add tinted color smoke to the standard white already being used. Britain's Air Ministry

showed interest in the basic apparatus with a view to military application for smoke-screening army or naval maneuvers from the air. One outcome of this official adoption of Savage's basic idea was to become a normal adjunct to the many RAF displays of the 1930s up until today's spectacular, immaculate precision flying, trailing colored smoke, by such aerobatic teams as the RAF's Red Arrows.

The 1920s saw the beginning of a continuing search for the aerial equivalent of the family automobile – a cheap-to-run, easy-to-fly, light sporting airplane design – which would, at least theoretically, put flying within the reach of the ordinary man. Low-powered engines were a prerequisite, allied to inexpensive construction which could be maintained with minimal engineering facilities and knowledge. Many splendid aircraft evolved from such a formula by the mid-1930s, a notable example being the long line of De Havilland Moth biplanes, but these hardly qualify as stunt or exhibition aircraft. One design which did border on the freakish, and became something of a craze for a few years, was the French pioneer Henri Mignet's notorious *Pou du Ciel* (Flying Louse or Flying Flea) which first appeared in September 1933. A low-powered, homemade design, the Flea cost a mere 1300 francs (about £20 then) for its complete airframe, plus a suitable engine costing from £35 to £50. The original engine used by Mignet in his first Flea was a simple 20-hp inverted twin Aubier-et-Dunne two-stroke unit, though later models employed various power units. Running costs were claimed to be as low as about two pence per mile. Flea clubs sprang into existence all over Britain by 1936, as non-pilots, blissfully believing the owner's claims that anyone could fly his masterpiece, eagerly constructed their family aircraft. Tragically, a high proportion of these never flew, while the number of fatalities among Flea pilots soon condemned the design as basically unstable and dangerous to fly.

Left: The Bucker *Jungmeister* (Young Champion), designed in 1935, and Germany's equivalent of the DH Tiger Moth, is a widely popular aerobatics aircraft.
Below left: Arrow Active, G-ABVE, was constructed in 1932 and was then flown in the 1932 and 1933 King's Cup Air Races.
Below: A Pitts S-2A Special, with the front cockpit faired over.

While those who could afford the luxury joined the many private flying clubs which mushroomed soon after World War I, a majority of the population of Britain had to be content with being simply spectators at the host of displays and air fairs which were organized in abundance each year. At such aerial exhibitions many thousands lined up to pay a reasonable sum for a brief flight around the adjacent countryside in ancient Avro 504s or other freelance aircraft, and one of the first ex-wartime pilots to make a living in this manner was Alan Cobham. Before long, Cobham had graduated from freelance to air-taxi operations, and then began to establish himself as one of the leading long-distance pioneering fliers. After some years of global flights and surveys for the newly created Imperial Airways' future intercontinental routes, Cobham turned his attention to the United Kingdom, flying a complete tour of Britain in a DH 61 Giant Moth titled *Youth of Britain* in his bid to make Britain air minded. From this idea grew the now-famous 'Cobham Circus': a travelling air show of – eventually – a dozen or so different types of aircraft which offered air displays and passenger flips at two or three different towns every week during the summer months. Undoubtedly, Cobham's Circus provided the baptism of the air for many hundreds of young men and boys which led to these latter taking up flying as a career in later years, and, incidentally, joining the RAF in the late 1930s. Cobham was later to pioneer air-to-air refuelling techniques which are now accepted as standard by a dozen military air forces of the world.

By the mid-1930s the day of the true barnstormer was over; civil aviation was being gradually enmeshed in a strangling spider web of rules, regulations, restrictions as bureaucracy gained the upper hand. No longer could an individual pilot simply take off and fly anywhere at will; aircraft were not permitted to be flown unless rigid standards of airworthiness had been checked, rechecked, inspected and rubber-stamped as fulfilling the requirements of paper rules of safety. Public air displays became carefully, meticulously planned affairs and the sheer *joie de vivre* spirit of the pioneering performers was quietly but firmly channelled along overregulated lines. In Britain the outstanding annual air display became that provided by the Royal Air Force at Hendon – the site of Claude Grahame-White's exhibitions decades before. The very first RAF Aerial Pageant had been held at Hendon on 3 July 1920 and for the next 18 years this annual RAF 'taxpayers' benefit' (its private nickname in the Service) was the greatest military flying exhibition in the world. The title was changed to RAF Display in 1925, but the high standards achieved in formation and aerobatic flying never altered except to improve in precision and apparent daring year by year. The final, and greatest, Display was held in 1937, and with one exception all 18 Displays were free of fatal accidents, and no member of the public was hurt.

Right: **Two members of the still-flourishing Tiger Club – devotees of the classic DH Tiger Moth – give a cloud-hanger's view of Redhill Aerodrome in Surrey, 1965.**
Far Right: **Another regular stunt in the pre-1939 era was 'tied-together' formation aerobatics, demonstrated here by three Gloster Gladiators of 87 Squadron, RAF.**
Below: **Crazy flying at zero height is a regular item at RAF Displays and is illustrated here by two Avro 504N Lynx.**

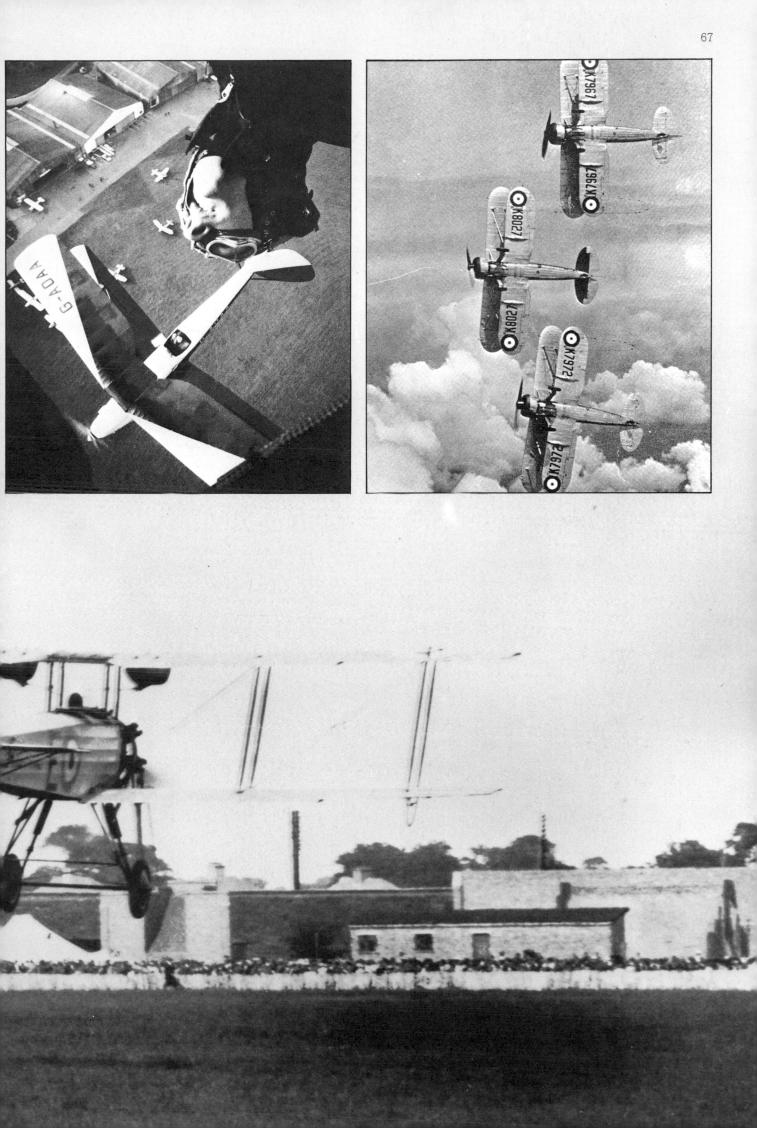

Hell's Angels

With the 1914–18 aerial war still fresh in memory, the world's cinematic industry was quick to exploit the pseudoglamour of the airplane in combat. Silent films in stark black and white tones began to appear based very loosely upon the lives of the wartime fliers, both real and fictional. One of the earliest was a German film titled simply *Richthofen*, which offered a highly imaginative version of the life and death of Germany's leading fighter ace, Rittmeister Manfred von Richthofen – the so-termed 'Red Baron.' The film's financial budget was small, its script a travesty of truth, yet it had at least the saving grace of featuring authentic wartime Fokker Dr1 triplanes, Albatros D Scouts, De Havilland 9 two-seat bombers and a genuine Nieuport 17 Scout. In the United States in the immediate post-bellum era there were several hundreds of genuine wartime aircraft, of more than 50 different design types; indeed, the US Army and US Navy air services then included several regular squadrons flying SE5as, Nieuport 28s, Spads, DH4s and even Fokker D VIIs. Against a backdrop of national pulp magazines trumpeting incredible deeds by American pilots and the burgeoning romantic mystique being fostered about knightly German fighter aces of World War I, a series of decidedly low-budget aerial films was hastily produced, including such forgettable epics as *Captain Swagger*, starring Rod La Rocque, and *The Lone Eagle*, featuring Raymond Keane.

If such early efforts suffered from banal scripts and plots and cliche acting, all possessed the advantage of readily available surplus, airworthy aircraft of the war era. Dozens of British, French, American and German biplanes of 1917–18 origin were pressed into celluloid service, usually bearing garish and improbable paint markings but authentic in overall structure and thereby successfully recreating a genuine esoteric atmosphere of aerial combat. Such veterans merely required the addition of some form of smoke-making apparatus to simulate burning victims, plus pure Hollywood armament, to appear very convincing to a younger generation of moviegoers already

Right: Two of 'Leutnant von Bruen's' Fokker *staffel* in *Hell's Angels* over California, 1928, a pair of the genuine D VIIs flown in the film.
Below: Frank Tomick (left) and E Burton Steene alongside the camera-equipped Travel Air 'Fokker' used for close-ups in *Hell's Angels*, at an airstrip near Chatsworth. Steene also filmed most aerial shots in later films, including *Wings* and *Legion of the Condemned*.

Above: Roy Wilson in an SE5a with 'Hollywood' armament, in *Hell's Angels*.
Below: The Sikorsky S-29a in its 'Gotha' livery for *Hell's Angels*, at Caddo Field, Van Nuys.
Right: The camera rig added to the nose of the Sikorsky 'Gotha' in *Hell's Angels* for close-ups of Ben Lyon in the front gunner's cockpit. Phil Jones, who died in the subsequent crash of this aircraft, is in the center, holding a tool box.

steeped in legends of the *Escadrille Lafayette* and German 'Knights of the Air.'

In 1926, however, filming commenced on the first true air epic, *Wings*. Directed by William Wellman, himself an ex-World War I pilot, and starring Buddy Rogers, Richard Arlen, Clara Bow (the 'It' girl, as she was publicized), and in a bit part a youngster named Gary Cooper, *Wings* was produced by the Paramount Studios and finally cost two million dollars in the making. It was first released in August 1927, and in the following year was accorded the honor of the Film Academy's very first Oscar award. Given the use of the US Army's Kelly Field, Texas, and Brooks Field, Wellman set about assembling a mini air force of some 220 aircraft – about 50 of these being genuine 1918 designs – and some 300 pilots. The bulk of the latter were regular serving US Army fliers, including a young officer named Hoyt Vandenberg, but for the more hazardous flying sequences Wellman hired a small band of professional stunt fliers. One of these daredevil civilian pilots was Dick Grace, a noted stunt pilot, who was to perform four separate 100-mph deliberate crashes as directed. A firm devotee of the calculated risk, Grace had the cockpit of a Spad single-seater reinforced with heavy steel tubing and invented a harness-type safety belt. The undercarriage struts were deliberately weakened, and the fuel tank held just enough fuel for a takeoff and brief flight. Over the mock battleground, Grace put the Spad into a dive toward the specially prepared patch of ground onto which he was required to crash, dipped the port wing into the earth, wiped off his undercarriage and turned turtle. Dazed but uninjured, Grace crawled out of the wreckage – only to discover a cedar log rammed into the fuselage just behind the cockpit, less than a foot from where his head had been!

His fourth crash for the cameras was in a Fokker D VII. Picking his spot carefully, Grace dived the Fokker into the ground, but the undercarriage failed to shear and Grace's head smashed into the instrument panel, breaking his neck. His luck still held – he survived to fly again many months later. The aircraft used in *Wings* were a motley mixture of authentic 1918 machines and suitably modified postwar types. These included Thomas Morse MB3s, Curtiss P1s, Vought VE-7s,

Martin MB2s and DH4s, each heavily camouflaged in dubious markings and color schemes. Aerial camera work was accomplished mainly from the open cockpits of the DH4s and Martins, and the chief cameraman was Harry Perry, who personally undertook some 50 flights in the course of filming. Though eventually released for the general public as a silent film, *Wings* was initially shown with a crude form of mechanically contrived sound effects to its actual battle scenes. A second innovation was the tinting of whole scenes in solid blue, yellow or red coloring, with such items as machine-gun bursts and burning aircraft *hand*-painted on every individual positive print of the film!

Among the first audience to view *Wings* was a 23-year-old Texan, Howard Hughes, a serious aviation devotee who had recently invested a small chunk of his vast personal fortune in two minor Hollywood films showing a 50-percent profit. *Wings* gave Hughes the final spur to his private ambition to make the greatest aerial film epic possible; accordingly he hired the producer Marshall Neilan and writer Joseph Moncure March, and began filming at the end of October 1927. The stars of his film were to be Ben Lyon from Warner Brothers, James Hall

from Paramount and a young Norwegian girl, Greta Nissen – all initially contracted for just three months' filming. At the end of that first three months Hughes had spent half a million dollars and had all the purely dramatic scenes 'in the can' – but had yet to film a single flying sequence. Since money was of no object to Hughes, he next set about acquiring a total of 87 miscellaneous aircraft – Fokker D VIIs, SE5as, Thomas Morse Scouts and a lumbering twin-engined Sikorsky S-29A owned by Roscoe Turner. Then he built a flying field at Inglewood, California – site of the later Los Angeles Airport – and hired a staff of mechanics to run the repair and construction sheds. He needed pilots. Instead of asking the US Army for help here, as Wellman had done, Hughes assembled his own band of civilian pilots – virtually every barnstormer or stunt pilot holding a current pilot's license then available. As chief pilot he hired Frank Clarke who gathered together the cream of Hollywood stunt fliers – men like his close buddy Frank Tomick, Al Wilson, Leo Nomis, Ira Reed, 'Phil' Phillips, Al Johnson and Roscoe Turner. Each man's basic salary was $200 per week, with negotiated bonuses for special stunts.

The film was titled *Hell's Angels* and the saga of its making epitomizes the skill and daring of those unpublicized stunt pilots of the 1920s and 1930s who continually risked life and limb in obsolete and one-off rebuilt aircraft for Hollywood's movie moguls. First in a series of accidents was Hughes himself, when he took off in a Thomas Morse Scout in a power climbing turn and almost immediately spun straight into the ground. Hughes walked away from the crash but several of

Below: Dick Grace, dressed for his part in *Wings*, stands by the nose of a 'converted' Thomas Morse scout.
Bottom: Some of the leading personalities in *Hell's Angels* are, from the left: Ralph Douglas, Leo Nomis, Frank Clarke, James Hall and Ben Lyon (stars of the film), Frank Tomick, and Roy Wilson. Behind the group is a genuine Sopwith Snipe.
Right: Some of the pilots, mechanics and cameramen for *Hell's Angels*, pose in front of the Sikorsky 'Gotha' fuselage. Roscoe Turner is at the extreme left, standing.

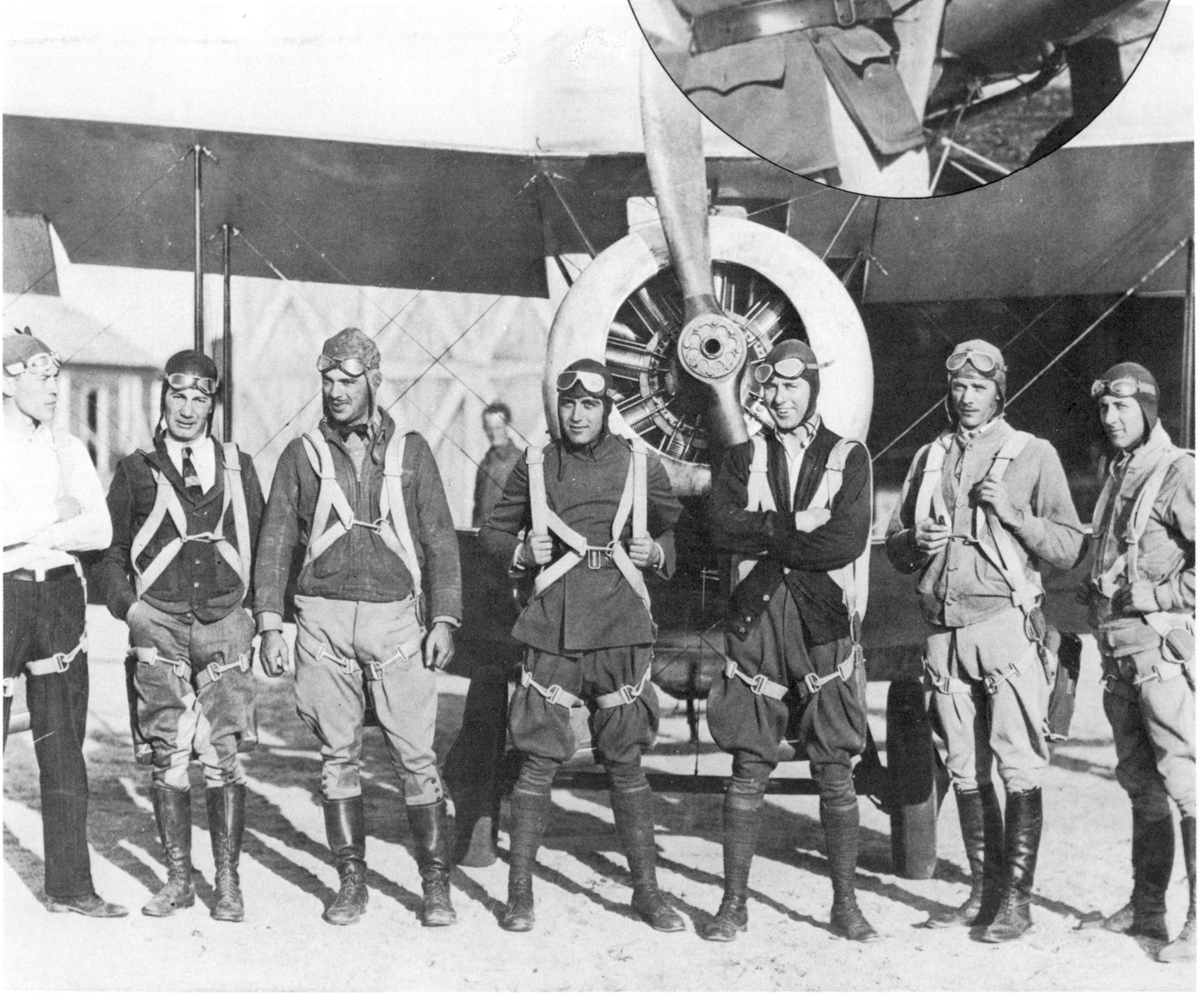

his hired pilots were not so fortunate. Al Johnson hit the earth with a wing-tip during a low pass but survived. Ross Cooke wrote off an SE5a at Santa Paula but lived. Then Al Johnson, in another SE5a, hit some high tension cables when taking off from Glendale Airport and died in the resulting explosion. Al Wilson, piloting a Fokker D VII over a Hollywood suburb, was treated to the sight of his propeller falling off and took to his parachute, the pilotless D VII eventually plowing into the ground just behind the house of a motion-picture magnate Joe Schenk. Then came a second fatality when C K 'Phil' Phillips in an SE5a got lost en route to location and ran out of fuel. The SE dived straight into the ground, killing Phillips. Three original Fokker D VIIs were wrecked beyond repair in various forced landings, while Roscoe Turner at the controls of his Sikorsky nearly spun into the ground near the San Bernardino mountains while delivering the huge aircraft to its film location. Shortly after, the Sikorsky failed to stop during a filmed takeoff sequence and crashed into the cameras, almost killing the camera crews and ending up in a bean field.

Air filming sequences – shot at eight different locations – were hugely realistic, having been shot from cameras mounted fore and aft of the cockpits of Fokkers flown by Roy Wilson and Frank Clarke, thereby ensuring absolute authenticity in all combat flying close-ups. The climax of this aerial artistry came near the end of the film when a sprawling dogfight was to be staged. For this it was decreed that the backdrop had to be a large nimbus cloudscape and, in October 1928, 40 pilots, 60 technicians and all associated aircraft and equipment were moved to Oakland Airport to shoot the dogfight. Here clear skies and blinding sunlight prevailed for weeks before filming could begin – indeed, it was to be four months before the sequence was finally completed.

The film plot called for the Sikorsky, heavily disguised as a German Gotha and crewed by Ben Lyon and James Hall ostensibly, to bomb a German munitions depot, only to be set upon by Von Richthofen's Circus, which in turn was to be engaged by an Allied fighter squadron. The Circus flew Fokker D VIIs – including a genuine example nearest camera – while the Allied squadron flew SE5as and Sopwith Camels (modified Thomas Morse Scouts). The result was a furious, wheeling, 31-aircraft dogfight which has never been surpassed for realism in any subsequent film – and without any film trickery or process faking. In the maelstrom of hair-raising near-misses and close encounters, Ira Reed and Stuart Murphy actually collided head-on, a sequence retained in the eventual public release edition. The ultimate scene concerned the shooting down of the Sikorsky Gotha by Von Richthofen's Fokker D VII. Though piloted by Roscoe Turner for all the bombing and dogfight scenes, for this last scene the Sikorsky was piloted by Al Wilson, and hidden in the rear fuselage was a mechanic, Phil Jones, to pump out smoke from a mixture of lamp black and flour via a smoke pot to simulate burning. Starting at 7000 feet, Wilson put the 'doomed Gotha' into a deliberate spin and Jones began making smoke. As the ground loomed uncomfortably large Wilson attempted to bring the aircraft out of its spin, but quickly realized this would be impossible. Yelling to Jones to

74

bale out, Wilson took to his parachute, but Jones evidently failed to react in time and perished in the subsequent crash.

Originally conceived as a silent film, *Hell's Angels* was converted for sound before release. This necessitated in the interim replacement of the heroine Nissen with her unintelligible accented 'English' by an American blonde bit-player named Harleen Carpenter – she was promptly renamed Jean Harlow by Hughes. The premiere of *Hell's Angels* was held on 27 May 1930 at Grauman's Chinese Theater, when an estimated multitude of more than one million people witnessed the extravagantly star-studded spectacle. The film's final cost was well over four million dollars and had taken more than two years to complete. Some two million feet of film had been exposed, 137 pilots and a like number of technicians had been employed, and four men had been killed. The result was without question all that Howard Hughes had hoped for – the great-

est aerial film epic ever made, a claim which still holds good despite the huge advances made in cinematography ever since.

The success of *Hell's Angels* sparked off a mini-flood of subsequent aerial theme films, among them *Sky Devils*, *Cock of the Air*, *Suzy*, *Lilac Time*, *Crimson Romance*, *Army Surgeon*, *Ace of Aces*, *Hell in the Heavens*, *The Eagle and the Hawk* and the original version of *Dawn Patrol*, made in 1930 and starring Richard Barthelmess and Douglas Fairbanks, Jr. In most of these the piloting was undertaken by Hollywood's stunt fliers with an apparently inevitable chapter of accidents and near-misses with death. During the filming of *Dawn Patrol* the veteran Earl Robinson almost lost his life when a dynamite charge simulating a bomb explosion was prematurely detonated right under Robinson's aircraft, nearly wrecking the machine and pilot. A remake of *Dawn Patrol* followed in 1938, starring Errol Flynn and David Niven, but apart from various studio close-ups

of the fresh stars in dummy cockpits et al, the aerial scenes were identical to the original version. The story was revamped into yet another version just after World War II, but was retitled as *Fighter Squadron*.

Many of the follow-up films after *Hell's Angels* simply edited in many flying scenes from the Hughes' production rather than expend large sums on creating their own aircraft sequences, but in 1938 yet another epic air film commenced when William Wellman directed *Men with Wings*, a tale of American aviation progress from 1903 to 1937. Starring Fred MacMurray and Ray Milland, it was a full technicolor production and thus required completely fresh aircraft and background sets. By then authentic 1918 machines were scarce. The only genuine Fokker D VII still available in the United States was acquired, then stripped to its 'bones' and completely rebuilt, including a more modern

Above: The genuine Pfalz D XII in its markings for *Dawn Patrol* at Newhall, California, in 1930. Later acquired by Colonel G B Jarrett for his vintage collection, the Pfalz was later still refurbished and owned by Frank Tallman.
Below: One of the Travel Air 'Wichita Fokkers' used in *Men with Wings* is pictured at Van Nuys Airport in 1938. The radiator was a dummy structure.

engine driving and all-metal propeller. Readily available, however, were a number of Travel-Air biplanes which, with suitable modification, could be converted into reasonable facsimile Fokkers. Indeed, the conversion design, undertaken by Lloyd Stearman at Wichita, led to these movie Fokkers acquiring the soubriquet 'Wichita Fokkers' thereafter. Other biplanes assembled for the film included an authentic Nieuport 28, Thomas Morse Scouts, a DH4, a Garland Lincoln, some Curtiss JN4 Jennies, a completely reconstructed Spad S VII Scout and a genuine Pfalz D XII, owned by Buck Kennel, which was brought up to flying state but in the event not used in filming.

For the flying sequences of *Men with Wings* Wellman assembled a crew of pilots from the Association of Motion Picture Pilots – the trade union of Hollywood's veteran stunt pilots. These included Frank Clarke, Herb White, 'Tex' Rankin, 'Chubby' Gordon, Walt Quinton, Ray Crawford, Stan Hicks, Bob Blair and the film's technical director Paul Mantz. Most of the key action close-ups were flown by Clarke and Mantz, and on one occasion while formating closely their aircraft momentarily locked wings. Only the pilots' superlative skill averted a double tragedy. Shortly after, while piloting a Boeing P-12 fighter for a later sequence, Mantz again brushed with death when he failed to pull out of a high-speed dive at the ground cameras at the planned height and only succeeded in doing so when literally within inches of the ground. Several other accidents and forced landings took their toll of the aircraft but caused no fatalities among the pilots. The outcome was a film with some spectacular flying scenes – and all in glorious technicolor.

Men with Wings was virtually the last full-scale aerial film involving World War I flying for more than two decades, although several attempts to recreate similar epics, such as Wellman's *Escadrille Lafayette*, appeared yet found little public favor. Then in 1965 in Eire, filming commenced on an adaption of a novel by Jack D Hunter, *The Blue Max*, produced by Twentieth Century Fox. Its theme was that of a ruthlessly ambitious German fighter pilot in 1917–18 and his obsession with winning the gallantry award, the *Pour Le Merite* (Blue Max). Based at Baldonnel, a film fleet of 25 aircraft were brought

together, including two Fokker Dr1 triplanes, three Fokker D VIIs, two Pfalz D IIIs and two SE5as. These 1918 designs had been constructed variously in Germany, Britain and France, while more modern biplanes were co-opted and drastically modified into a semblance of World War I outline including DH Tiger Moths, Caudrons and Stampes. The leading role of Leutnant Bruno Stachel was acted by the American George Peppard, who did much of the routine flying required. For the more dangerous dogfighting, hedge-hopping and crash-landing sequences his place in the cockpit was taken by a slim, short – just five feet, two inches – lady pilot Joan Hughes, who had first flown at the age of 15 and was an ex-wartime ATA ferry pilot. With the benefits of full color and Cinemascope, and width screening, *The Blue Max* – despite a mundane

Left: A 'Fokker D VII' is hotly pursued by a Spad S VII in a frame from *Men with Wings*. The smoke-making pipes can be seen at the side of the fuselage extending underneath.
Below: Travel Air (Hisso engine) is suitably disguised as a 'Fokker D VII' for *Men with Wings* in 1938.

script – offered some superb flying episodes, recreating much of the charisma of 1918 aerial combat.

A number of the pre-1939 Hollywood flying veterans who provided aerial thrills for millions of moviegoers continued flying until old age or a natural death took their hands from the control columns. Several died 'in harness,' still displaying a skill acquired over many years of hard-won experience, flirting with death or mutilation. Frank Clarke, the 'Von Bruen' of *Hell's Angels*, was killed while flying in 1948, and his death was witnessed by his closest friend, Frank Tomick, who then gave up flying forever. Paul Mantz, probably the peer of more modern aviation films, also died in front of a camera; he was killed in an air crash in July 1965 while flying in the making of the film *Flight of the Phoenix*. Such men had devoted their lives to aviation, no less than the highly publicized pioneers and record-breakers of the golden years of flying. They had calmly accepted risks and dangers daily to provide a sensation-hungry public with thrills, but their epitaph is a heritage of courage and skill now being embellished by the latest generation of movie pilots.

Higher, Faster, Farther

Once having accomplished heavier-than-air flight, man followed his instinctive, restless passion for progression to the ultimate. In the context of aviation this was translated into continuing intensive attempts to reach higher speeds, greater altitudes and longer ranges. By the outbreak of war in 1914 – a mere 11 years on from the first pioneering hops by the Wright brothers – airplanes were already reaching speeds well in excess of 100 mph, heights above 20,000 feet, and distances that shrank the hitherto land barriers of nations. Safety and crew comfort were of secondary importance – performance was all. The war escalated certain facets of aircraft performance, particularly in steady improvement of aero engines, and under the stress of operational conditions crews often ventured higher

and faster than the arbitrary parameters of design performance stipulated by manufacturers. The rules of flying were still in the main empirical; only hard experience taught the answers to a myriad problems.

By the time of the November 1918 cessation of hostilities certain aircraft had achieved limits only dreamed of by the prewar pioneers. Maximum speeds of several designs were in the 130–140-mph band, and ceilings of 25–30,000 feet not unknown; the latest heavy bombers about to enter service were confidently expected to be capable of carrying a full war load from East Anglia in England to Berlin, bomb and return to base. Designers of most nations had already explored the advantages of cantilever wing construction, thereby blazing a trail to eventual domination of monoplane configuration in aeronautics, yet the contemporary aviation scene still firmly belonged to the trusted, proven biplane. While the peace heralded the hope of a new age for mankind, conversely it brought aeronautical advance to a swift halt, albeit temporarily. At the close of 1918 all nations possessed stocks of aircraft numbered in thousands – with, incidentally, even greater numbers of men trained to fly them – and aircraft manufacturers were permitted to continue fulfilling a proportion of wartime production contracts for several months in order to ease the

Right: A replica of a Vickers Vimy in the RAF Museum, Hendon, built in 1969 to mark the fiftieth anniversary of Alcock and Brown's nonstop crossing of the Atlantic in June 1919.
Below: The American Navy Curtiss NC-4 flying boat, commanded by Lieutenant Commander A C Read, USN, achieved the first trans-Atlantic aerial crossing – by stages – in May 1919.

80

Alcock and Brown's Vickers Vimy in an Irish bog at the end of its trans-Atlantic direct crossing on 15 June 1919. At the far left is a Bristol F2b which attempted to land alongside but also fell victim to the boggy field.

general employment of labor situation. Such an abundance of existing airplanes, added to a worldwide revulsion of any item pertaining to war, logically nullified any governmental financial support for fresh experimentation in airplane design or advancement, leaving any immediate furtherance of aeronautics to individual enthusiasts or private firms.

To the dyed-in-the-wool aviation enthusiasts the coming of peace was a double relief; now they could pick up the traces of prewar projects and proceed without 'outside' hindrance. One prime target for such men was the prize of £10,000 originally offered in April 1913 by Lord Northcliffe, proprietor of the *Daily Mail*, to the first person or persons to fly nonstop across the Atlantic Ocean. Though suspended when war commenced the following year, the offer was renewed by Northcliffe in July 1918 and officially sanctioned as an open competition on 15 November 1918. The few conditions imposed upon entrants included a time limit of 72 hours for the overall crossing, allowance for one open-seas landing only, no 'enemy aircraft' designs to partake and the pilot was *not* to be a member of the Services. The Vickers firm already had an airplane which they confidently declared could 'fly the 1880 miles in about 20 hours from St Johns, Newfoundland, to Valencia' – the Vimy bomber of 1918. On 11 March 1919 a wartime bomber pilot, demobilized from the RAF only 24 hours before, walked into the Vickers' offices and quickly convinced the firm's management that he was the pilot they needed. He was Captain John Alcock, 27 years old and a pre-1914 test pilot. In the same month Arthur Whitten-Brown, an ex-RAF observer, applied for an engineer's post with Vickers and, by pure chance during his interview, was asked if he could navigate an aircraft across the Atlantic. On replying in the affirmative, Brown was immediately given the post of Alcock's navigator. The aircraft

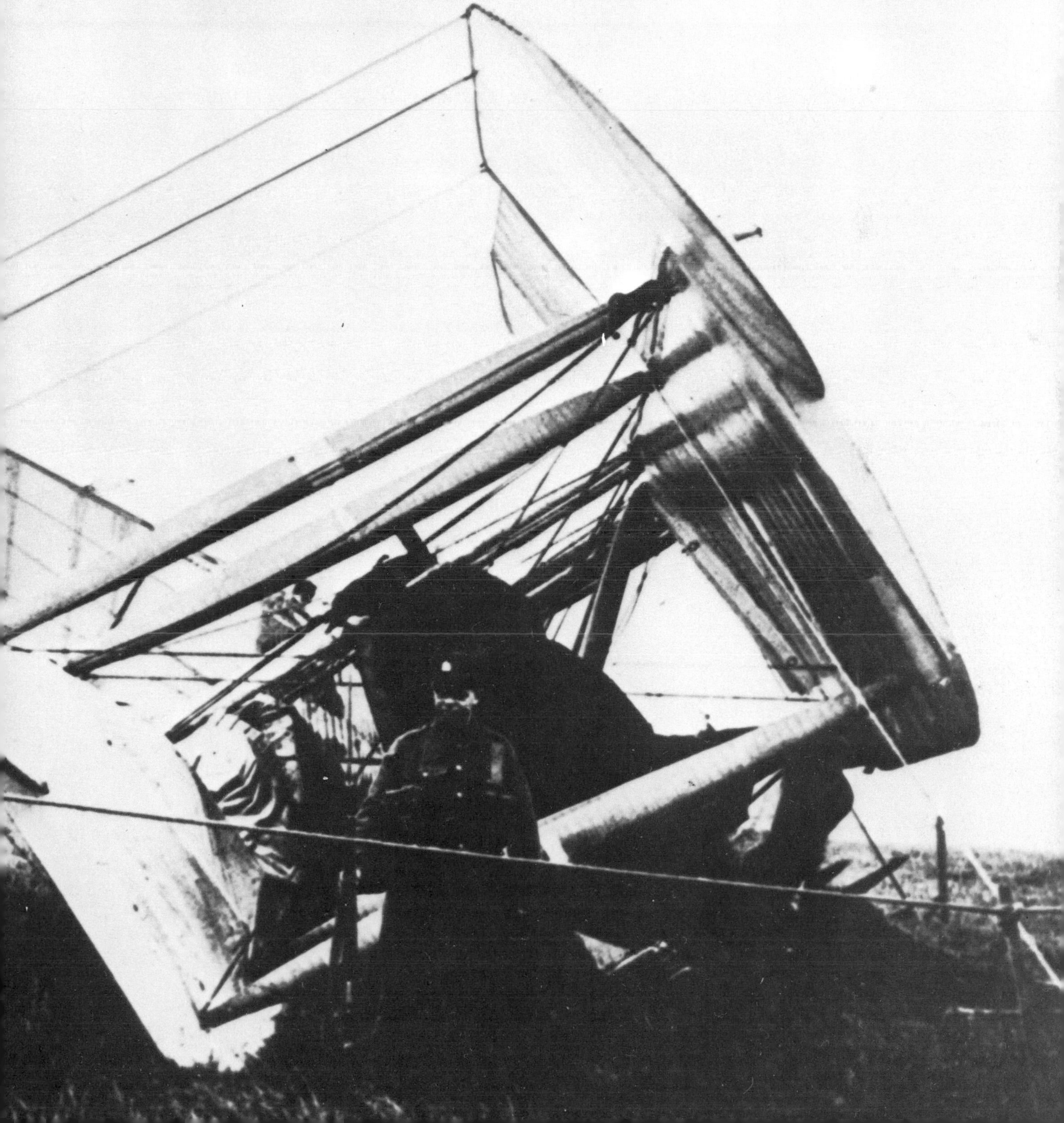

Above: Keith Ross-Smith (left of the trio in the cockpit) and his crew inspect the Vimy G-EAOU prior to his England-to-Australia flight, 1919.

Below: F S Cotton and W A Townsend in their DH 14A, G-EAPY, at Hendon on 2 February 1920, about to attempt the first London-to-Cape Town flight. In the event, the aircraft crashed at Messina, Italy, in a forced landing.

selected for the attempt was the thirteenth production machine then being shaped at Vickers, while the team chosen to carry out the entire Vimy program totalled 13, from Alcock to the general handyman assistant – ominous figures for those who thrive on superstition!

Transferred in toto to Newfoundland within weeks, the pale yellow Vimy finally left the New World soil at 1345 hours (local time) on 14 June 1919, and 15 minutes later left the Newfoundland coast behind and headed out over the vast Atlantic. Fifteen hours and 57 minutes later, having survived momentous storms, freezing icing-up of the whole aircraft, and a large part of the trip without sight of stars to navigate by or sea to calculate height from, the Vimy and its fatigued two-man crew passed over the coastline of Eire. Fifteen minutes later, attempting to land, the Vimy dug its nose into an Irish bog close to the Marconi radio station at Clifden – the Atlantic had been truly conquered by air. Apart from various prize monies, both men were knighted on 21 June 1919; yet John Alcock was to wear his honors for only a brief period. Only six months later, on 18 December, when trying to land in a fog near Rouen, France, he crashed and was killed.

Two further prizes of £10,000 each were inaugurated in 1919 for long-distance pioneering flights. In March the Australian Government put up such a cash award for the first Australian nationals to complete an England-to-Australia flight within an elapsed period of 720 hours (30 days); the second check was offered by the *Daily Mail* for the first successful flight from Cairo, Egypt, to Cape Town, South Africa. For the first of these projects a four-man Australian crew was assembled, with Sir Ross Smith and his brother Sir Keith Smith as pilot and navigator respectively, and Sergeants J W Bennett and W H Shiers as mechanics. The aircraft selected was another Vickers Vimy standard bomber, civil-registered as G-EAOU – or 'God 'Elp All Of Us' as Ross Smith quipped. On 12 November the Vimy and its all-Australian crew left a bleak Hounslow airdrome (now the site of London's Heathrow Airport) and, after a series of stages – planned and unplanned – reached Darwin nearly 52 hours inside the stipulated 720, having covered 11,080 miles

Right: The Douglas World Cruiser No. 3, named *Boston*, is one of four DWCs which attempted the first round-the-world flight, commencing 6 April 1924. In the event, two DWCs failed to complete the flight (including this machine), but the other pair accomplished the record 'first' successfully.

Below right: Fairey IIID, A10-3, sold to the Australian government, in which Wing Commander S J Goble, RAAF and Flying Officer I E McIntyre, RAAF flew round the entire 8568 miles of the Australian coastline in 44 days (flying time approximately 90 hours). The crew was awarded the 1924 Britannia Trophy for this performance.

Below: Captain Lowell Smith and Lieutenant John Ritcher, in a modified DH4B, receiving fuel via a length of two-inch hose suspended beneath another DH4B (Lts Hine and Seifert) on 23 June 1923. Smith and Ritcher remained airborne for little more than 24 hours before a blocked fuel line forced them to land.

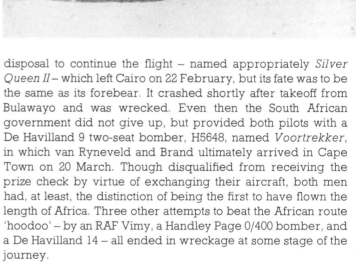

in an elapsed time of 668 hours and 20 minutes. The Vimy used was then taken to Adelaide, home town of Ross Smith, where it found its final, preserved resting place. Tragically, like John Alcock, Ross Smith lived for only a brief period after his momentous triumph, and died two years later.

The attempts to capture the prize offered for the Cairo-Cape flight were a brief saga of courage and frustration. First to try were two wartime Sopwith Camel nightfighter pilots, Captains F C Broome and S Cockerell, flying a Vimy-Commercial registered G-EAAV, suitably modified internally to accommodate extra fuel tankage. Carrying three 'passengers,' the Vimy-Commercial left Brooklands on 24 January 1920 for Cairo. There, early in the morning of 6 February, they started off on the projected flight to South Africa. By 27 February, after no few trials and tribulations, they reached Tabora, Tanganyika, but on that date as they took off on the next leg, to Abercorn, Rhodesia, engine failure shortly after takeoff led to a crash-landing which completely wrecked the aircraft. The South African government rose to the occasion by sponsoring its own attempt to gain the *Daily Mail* prize. It chose a Vimy and had its entire airframe doped in aluminum silver – hence *Silver Queen* – and engaged two ex-wartime South African aces, Lieutenant-Colonel Pierre van Ryneveld and Major C J Quintin Brand, plus two mechanics to crew the machine. Leaving Cairo just before midnight on 10 February 1920 – van Ryneveld hoped to fly all stages by night in cooler air – the *Silver Queen* experienced engine failure and was wrecked in a forced landing at Kurusku, only 530 miles from Cairo. Undismayed, a second Vimy was then placed at van Ryneveld's

disposal to continue the flight – named appropriately *Silver Queen II* – which left Cairo on 22 February, but its fate was to be the same as its forebear. It crashed shortly after takeoff from Bulawayo and was wrecked. Even then the South African government did not give up, but provided both pilots with a De Havilland 9 two-seat bomber, H5648, named *Voortrekker*, in which van Ryneveld and Brand ultimately arrived in Cape Town on 20 March. Though disqualified from receiving the prize check by virtue of exchanging their aircraft, both men had, at least, the distinction of being the first to have flown the length of Africa. Three other attempts to beat the African route 'hoodoo' – by an RAF Vimy, a Handley Page 0/400 bomber, and a De Havilland 14 – all ended in wreckage at some stage of the journey.

Elsewhere in the world a host of individual pilots were also tempting fate and the elements, flying to the limits of their machines and carving out air trails which in years to come would become regular passenger routes. Less glamorous yet vital pioneering flights were also made in conveying air mail across continents and between nations; communication was established by air in a fraction of the time hitherto accomplished by the traditional land and sea routes. The airplane was 'shrinking' the globe. Proof of this was afforded by a particularly outstanding duration flight undertaken in 1924 by four American Douglas DWC (Douglas World Cruisers). Leaving Seattle, Washington, on 6 April, all four DWCs headed northward to Alaska where the flagplane (named *Seattle*) crashed into a mountain, though the crew survived. A second DWC (*Boston*) was forced to retire on reaching the Azores. The remaining

pair, *Chicago* and *New Orleans*, however, eventually completed their transglobal flight; they arrived back in Seattle on 28 September 1924 after flying a total mileage of 26,345 (42,398 km) in an elapsed time of 175 days, with an actual flying time of 363 hours and seven minutes. This prodigious flight had been virtually a succession of planned stages, with necessary stops en route for constant refuelling and maintenance. But the possibilities of long, sustained flight for great distances had already begun to be explored when, in 1923, two Americans, Captain L H Smith and Lieutenant J P Richter, set a world endurance record in an open cockpit De Havilland 4B of more than 37 hours. This had been made possible by air-to-air refuelling on 15 occasions throughout their flight.

Right: Amy Johnson's DH60G, Gipsy Moth G-AAAH, *Jason*, as it is today, preserved in London's Science Museum at Kensington.
Bottom: Fairey IIIDs of the RAF's first Cairo-to-Cape flight from 1 March to 21 June 1926, are seen here at Heliopolis on their return to Cairo.
Below: De Havilland 60G, Moth, G-AAAH, at Ismailia, Egypt, piloted by W L Hope during a flight from England to Kisumu, in September 1928. In May 1930 this Gipsy Moth, renamed *Jason* and piloted by Amy Johnson, flew from England to Australia – the first such flight by a woman solo.

In the realm of speed, international contests had existed since pre-1914 days. The prime competitions were the international Gordon Bennett airplane race inaugurated in America in October 1910 and the Jacques Schneider Air Racing Trophy for Hydro-airplanes – or Schneider Trophy as it became commonly titled – which was first contested at Monaco on 16 April 1913 over 28 laps of a 10-kilometer course. The latter contest was resumed after World War I and quickly gained recognition as the world's most coveted air speed trophy. After a void race at Bournemouth, England, in 1919, the first postwar contest was held at Venice in 1920, resulting in a win for Italy. The following year again saw Italy take first placing, but in 1922 at Naples Henri Biard of Britain flying a Supermarine Sea Lion II prevented the Italians gaining its third – and therefore permanent – win. In 1923, when the venue was Cowes on the southern English coast, the United States made its first entries when two Curtiss CR-3 biplanes took first and second places. America repeated this success in the 1925 race held at Baltimore when Lieutenant James 'Jimmy' Doolittle recorded a winning speed of 232.57 mph in his Curtiss R3C-2.

Though won by a biplane, the 1925 contest saw Britain for the first time enter a monoplane contestant, the Supermarine S.4 twin-float racing seaplane which, prior to the contest, had already claimed a world speed record of 226.752 mph. The ninth Schneider Trophy Contest, held at Hampton Roads, United States, in 1926, witnessed a straight fight between Italy and America – and between biplane and monoplane. The American team flew well-proven Curtiss R3Cs but Italy's pilots thundered around the course in Macchi M-39 monoplanes – and won. The fast biplane was to figure in only one more Schneider contest, in 1927 at Venice, when Flight Lieutenant S M Kinkead of the RAF High Speed Flight piloted a sleek Gloster IVb for six laps before a cracked airscrew boss forced his retirement. Kinkead's second lap of the sharply triangulated course had produced a speed of 277.1 mph – the fastest figure for any biplane ever participating in the contest to date – but by now the monoplane was supreme in this field.

If the biplane was not the most efficient configuration for the

88

attainment of ultimate airplane speed, its multisurfaces seemed ideal for exploration of the upper atmosphere. The physical problems of rising to great altitudes had been recognized even before the advent of the airplane – decreasing air pressure which could boil a man's blood above 11 miles, and reduction in oxygen content of the upper air which might suffocate the human frame. Other dangers included the bitter freezing temperatures – roughly 100 degrees Fahrenheit of frost at six or seven miles high – and the gradual disorientation of any unprotected pilot once out of reach of recognizable land-marks. Despite all such hazards there remained the inviting prospect of utilizing the reduced density of high-altitude air for greater speeds in international airline communications, an objective which, added to man's natural striving for bigger and better levels of attainment in any field of activity, inspired a series of attempts to conquer the stratosphere and beyond.

By 1918 many aircraft and crews had already reached heights of 15–20,000 feet and experienced the accompanying dis-comforts of oxygen lack and intense cold, coupled with the restriction of pure physical movement at such altitudes. The contemporary methods of aircraft construction did not lend themselves easily to incorporation of pressurized cockpits for high-altitude fliers; the first piercing of the stratosphere was not made until 1931 when a Swiss professor, Auguste Piccard, electrified the world by rising to an altitude of 51,458 feet. His vehicle had been an aluminum sphere supported by a giant balloon of 500,000 cubic feet capacity, and the whole venture had been meticulously planned and engineered on scientifi-cally calculated data. Exemplifying the airplane's bid to equal Piccard's feat was the successful capture of the world's height

Above: Howard Pixton and his Sopwith Schneider at Monaco, winners of that year's Schneider Trophy Contest.
Left: Breguet XIX TR *Bidon*, later named *Point d'Interrogation*, (Question Mark), in which the French crew Dieudonne Costes and Maurice Bellonte linked Paris and New York nonstop by airplane for the first time on 1–2 September 1930. It is now preserved in the Musée de l'Air.
Below: Alan Cobham's De Havilland 50J, G-EBFO, in which he made historic survey flights from England to the Cape and to Australia in the 1920s.

Above: Sopwith Schneider (450-hp Cosmos engine) built for the 1919 Schneider Trophy Contest and civil-registered as G-EAKI. Piloted by Harry Hawker, it was forced to retire from the race on the first lap of the Bournemouth course. Fitted with wheeled undercarriage, it was later used by Hawker for other races.
Left: American Curtiss R2C, A-6692 at Port Washington Island, New York, in September 1924. A winner in the American Pulitzer races (Lieutenant A J Williams), A-6692 was ordered to be modified for the 1924 Schneider Trophy Contest at Baltimore. In fact, this contest was sportingly cancelled by the US National Aeronautic Association when Britain and Italy failed to enter.

record for aircraft on 16 September 1932. On that date Cyril Uwins, chief test pilot for the Bristol Aeroplane firm, flew a Vickers Vespa biplane with a finely tuned Bristol Pegasus engine to an altitude of 43,976 feet, and from an open cockpit. Two years later, in a Caproni biplane, Renato Donati of Italy added nearly 4000 feet to Uwins' record, but was in a state of near-collapse when he finally returned to earth. Even this figure was surpassed in November 1935 when the Russian Vladimir Kokinaki managed to rise some 500 feet higher. Thereafter virtually all such climbs were flown by pressurized-cockpit monoplanes specifically designed for their purpose.

If the 1920s and early 1930s were indeed the golden years of adventure in the air in the context of greater achievements in

every sphere of aeronautics year by year, then the true spirit of that era was truly exemplified by the numerous individuals who undertook perilous ventures of their own volition, often without 'official' sponsorship or, occasionally, even approval. During little more than a decade from the mid-1920s, at a stage in aviation when the boundless freedom of the air had yet to be confined and restricted by a mountain of bureaucratic rules and regulations, a host of pilots, male and female, of widely varied experience, challenged raw nature and the gods of chance in the frail wood and fabric biplanes available by undertaking semiglobal flights. Among a galaxy of truly courageous pilots several individuals stand high above the ruck. Men like H J L 'Bert' Hinkler, the diminutive Australian-born son of a German immigrant, who came to England pre-1914 to seek his future in aviation. Serving with the RNAS from 1914 as a mechanic, then aerial gunner, Hinkler finally became a pilot in 1918, and in the same year dreamed of flying home to Australia, an ambition he was not to fulfill until 10 long, frustrating years later. Then, in a tiny Avro Avian biplane with only the barest necessities bought from his meager private funds, Hinkler set out from Croydon on 7 February 1928. Three weeks later, on 22 February, a weary Hinkler, sun-scorched, unshaven and desperately fatigued, eased the little Avian down at Darwin, having flown solo to Australia – the first man to accomplish such a feat. For the following five years 'Little Bert' added further laurels to his record-making efforts – always alone and usually without fuss or publicity beforehand – until he found a lonely death high in the Prato Magno Alps in the evening of 7 January 1933; it was the first stage of yet another attempted solo flight to his homeland from England.

The restless urge to push back the existing barriers of the airplane was exemplified by dozens of civil and Service crews, many of them paying with their lives for their daring. Men like the Frenchmen Charles Nungesser and Francois Coli, who set out from Le Bourget airdrome, Paris, on 8 May 1927 in their all-white Levasseur PL-8 *L'Oiseau Blanc* (The White Bird) attempting to cross the Atlantic – and were never seen again. Three years later, on 1 September 1930, another French duo took off from Le Bourget with the same objective. The following day their all-red Breguet XIX – cynically titled *Point d'Interrogation* (Question Mark) – arrived at Curtiss Field, New York, having covered 3700 miles in 37 hours 17 minutes. Nor was the aviation scene entirely male dominated. In the spring of 1928 Lady Heath flew an Avro Avian III, G-EBUG, from South Africa to London – the first such solo flight by a woman pilot; on 5 May 1930 Amy Johnson set out alone in a De Havilland 60G Gipsy Moth, G-AAAH, *Jason*, and nine days later reached Darwin, Australia – another first in the history of aviation but by no means the last. Such record feats attracted worldwide publicity and acclaim, yet behind the ballyhoo and ecstatic news media headlines many pilots were quietly laying the true foundations for the future of the airplane. In Britain the first national airline, Imperial Airways, was formed on 1 April 1924 with a mixed bag of 13 aircraft; exactly three months later the first regular transcontinental airmail service in the United States was inaugurated. If the airplane was to be acceptable to the layman public it had to be shown to be safe, reliable and capable of scheduled services. One man in particular, in Britain, who visualized a network of aerial routes linking every part of the British Empire was Alan Cobham. A wartime pilot, Cobham devoted his energies almost exclusively into helping to make the ordinary citizen air-minded by first creating an air-taxi service from 1921–23, and then pioneering many routes to India, South African and other overseas territories. Much of his work was deliberately planned as a survey of future passenger-carrying air services, and from 1925–28, flying landplanes, flying boats and float-planes, Cobham blazed many civil airline trails later to be established as regular routes. Thereafter Cobham became primarily associated with his Flying Circuses;

a barnstorming collection of all types of aircraft in which he afforded the opportunities for many thousands of the British public to pay for their first taste of flying as a passenger.

It was an era which gave birth to the many privately organized civil flying clubs. These organizations were made possible by a host of small, lightly powered biplanes produced especially for pleasure flight, aircraft epitomized by the appearance in February 1925 of the prototype De Havilland 60 'Moth' two-seat light biplane. This was the 'father' of a generation of functional, low-powered, easy-to-fly, light airplanes which remain popular even today for sporting and pure pleasure flying. The many derivatives of that original 'Moth' were responsible not only for a number of the most successful long-distance record flights of the period, but introduced many hundreds of would-be pilots to the upper air. Possibly the most famous, and certainly the most prolific, of later variants was the DH 82A 'Tiger Moth' which first flew in 1931. 'Tigers' were the principal ab initio trainers for the Royal Air Force for almost two decades and virtually all the RAF's wartime-trained crews during 1939–45. It was a heyday for private enterprise in airplane design and construction in every sense of the phrase, and led to the appearance of dozens of different cheap, low-powered aircraft from highly individual 'manufacturers.' Not all of them could be considered entirely safe or even airworthy, such was the growing demand by an enthusiastic public for reasonably priced flying. Tuition of an embryo civilian pilot was offered by a variety of private flying clubs for the relatively modest price of about £20 (approximately $80) to license-standard skill, usually in surroundings which often included full club facilities of hangarage, restaurant and bar, and an off-duty social calendar of events attended by other flying enthusiasts.

By the mid-1930s the rapidly advancing state of knowledge and comprehension of aeronautical expertise was dictating the virtual demise of the biplane's domination in design. Monoplane configurations offered greater speeds, longer range and higher operating altitude ceilings, with less intricate construction problems. Both in the civil and service fields the biplane was by then outmoded in concept, an anachronism in the ever-escalating graph of aerial progress and attainment. Though still in large evidence among the world's air forces, the future for the airplane clearly lay with the single-winged aircraft – in itself a form of reversal to man's earliest attempts to emulate the birds and mimic nature's most efficient exponents of flight.

Above: Two of the Gloster IVs prepared for the 1927 Schneider Trophy Contest in Venice, seen here at Calshot. The N223, foreground, was flown by Flight Lieutenant S M Kinkead in the race, achieving a third lap time of 277.1 mph – an all-time record for biplane types – before being forced to retire with a cracked propeller shaft. This marked the last appearance of biplanes in these contests.
Left: A De Havilland DH 60M 'Moth' VH-ULM from Australia.

Crashes

Left: An Avro 504 adds insult to injury.
Right: The giant Staaken VGO.II, R.9/15 after returning from a bombing sortie against a Russian rail station in late 1916. Running out of fuel, due to head winds, it force landed at Paulsgnade, near Mitau, with surprisingly light damage. At least the two gunners in the engine cupolas had a good view of the event!
Below: Avro 504b, No. 1042, which failed to get airborne with its bomb load from Imbros, in the Aegean, 1916. Fortunately for its pilot, the bombs failed to detonate.

NOTICE
NO RUBBISH
TO BE SHOT HERE.
BY ORDER.
D.O.R.E.

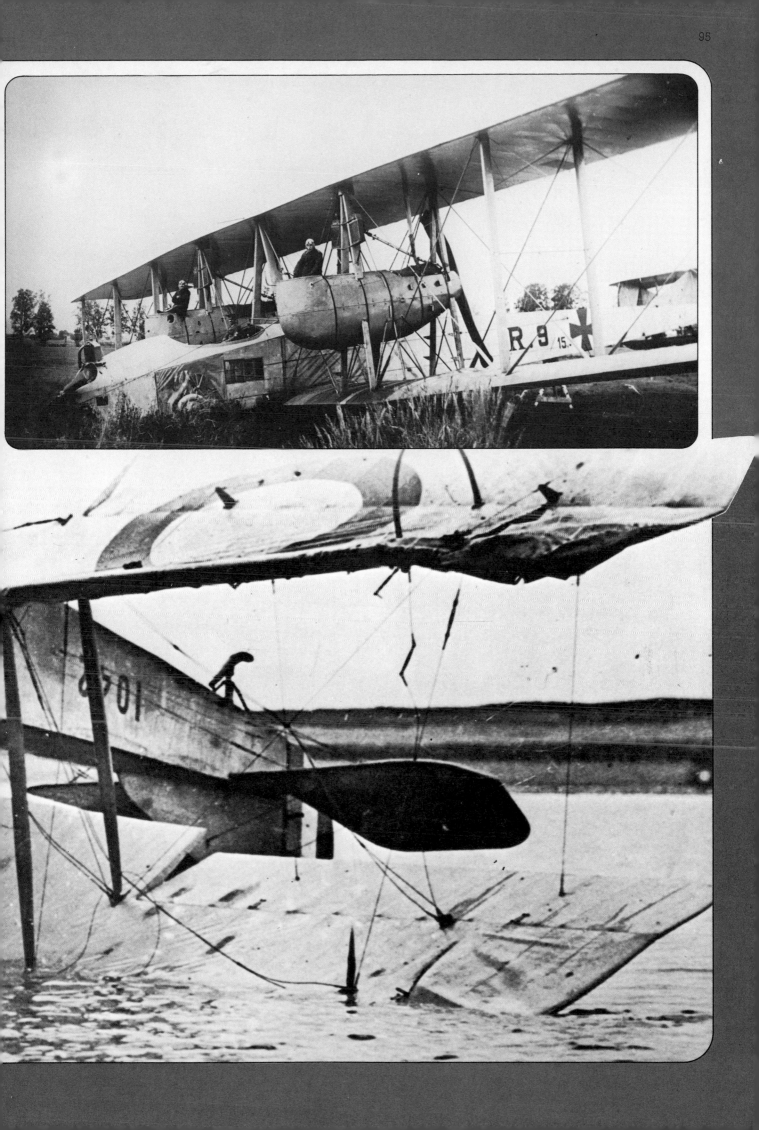

Left: Avro 504J of No. 52 (Training) Squadron, RFC on the roof of a cobbler's shop in Staines, Middlesex, in 1918.
Right: An American in the RFC, Lieutenant 'Loot' Harrison Brown, who tried to enter a hangar in his BE2e – without trying the door first.
Below: Sopwith Schneider Scout of RNAS Killingholme (No. 3768) in 1916.

98

Left: Pilot of 407 Flight, Fleet Air Arm and his Blackburn Dart, N9811, having literally missed the boat when attempting to land on an aircraft carrier.
Right: Handley Page 0/100, No. 1462 of 7A Squadron, RNAS at Villacoublay, France, after a taxiing mishap.

Below: A Ninak gets too friendly. Sergeant Walker of B Flight, 47 Squadron, RAF hits Flying Officer Coggle of A Flight during a formation landing of 47's DH9As at Helwan, Egypt, in 1926.

Left: Training casualties were prolific at every stage of ab initio instruction in every air force. These Hawker Harts of No. 9 Flying Training School Thornaby, RAF in 1937 tried to land on the same patch of turf.

Right: Short Syrinx, G-ACJK, at Evert, Brussels, on 9 October 1935, after being overturned by a gale. Repaired, it survived until 1940.

Below: A Supermarine Southampton, N9899, of 480 (CR) Flight which crashed on 4 June 1926, is seen here on Calshot's northern slipway.

Bottom: Flying Officer I V Hue Williams, RAF, while demonstrating his Avro Tutor, K4809 at the 1935 Hendon RAF Display in the comic role of a ham-fisted 'pupil,' landed just a little *too* low.

Sea-Boots

Man's inherent affinity with the oceans from which he evolved has been reflected over countless centuries in his conquest of the seas and rivers surrounding him in every environment. It was, therefore, a natural step in progress for him to attempt to apply his latest invention – aviation – to a maritime use. Based on a thirteenth-century theory of Roger Bacon that there existed an 'aerial ocean' upon which any flying vehicle could 'float,' subsequent notions and experiments for aerial carriages often included some form of man-carrying boat or vessel supported by whatever fanciful means of aerial locomotion dreamed up by its designer. Investigations and practical testing in the latter half of the nineteenth century gave promise for future designs of fast, efficient boat hulls for water-surface use, and much of the data and experience accumulated in these was to be put to good use when the initial flying-boat designs were considered. Once the Wright brothers had clearly demonstrated the feasibility of man-controlled, sustained flight in 1903, and the results of their patient, scientifically engineered efforts had begun to reach a wider audience, it was to be relatively little time before the first attempts to fly from a water surface.

As early as 1909 in Britain, E W Wakefield formed the Lakes Flying Company at Windermere with a declared purpose of building and flying maritime airplanes – or hydro-airplanes as as the first float-planes were dubbed. In France Henri Fabre accomplished the world's first takeoff from water at Martigues, near Marseille, on 28 March 1910. In Britain on 18 November 1911 Commander Oliver Schwann, RN, made his country's first flight from water in an Avro Type D biplane fitted with rudimentary floats, though his (then) lack of experience led to a subsequent crash-landing. In America Glenn H Curtiss, the first American after the Wright brothers to fly, began his own experiments with float-planes and boat hulls for his designs. Curtiss's deep interest and practical expertise in the progression of the true flying boat was to become the rock foundation of Britain's future maritime aircraft, particularly during 1914–18, but British designers in this field were already considering and building waterborne airplanes. The first British flying boat was built by T O M Sopwith in late 1912, a 'pusher' biplane construction superimposed upon a Saunders-built hydroplane hull and powered by a 90-hp Austro-Daimler engine. Titled Bat

Above left: Sopwith Bat Boat No. 1 of 1912, the world's first practical amphibian and Europe's first truly successful flying boat. The aircraft structure (wings etc) could be detached in toto from the boat hull.
Above: Curtiss H.12 'Large America' flying boat used by the RNAS.
Below: An FBA (Franco-British Aviation) flying boat, N1047, used widely as an RNAS trainer for flying-boat crews, is seen here at Calshot, Hampshire, on 1 September 1917, with Lieutenant Scott as pilot.

Above: Gotha Ursinus GUH UWD seaplane of early 1916, designed by Oskar Ursinus, editor of *Flugsport*. Only one seaplane version was built and it ended its days as a training machine for torpedo crews.

Right: The massive Felixstowe Fury, designed by John Porte, powered by five Rolls-Royce Eagle engines, with upper wings spanning 123 feet. Emerging in 1918, the Fury was mooted for a trans-Atlantic crossing, but was wrecked in Harwich Harbour on 11 August 1919.

Below: The Short S.14 *Sarafand* was completed in 1932 as an experiment in construction of truly large flying boats, with wings spanning 120 feet, and power from six 825-hp Rolls-Royce Buzzard II engines in tandem pairs. Only one example was built (S1589).

Boat No. 1, it was not only Europe's first *successful* flying boat, but arguably the world's first practical amphibian aircraft, having a pair of retractable wheels fitted alongside the hull in 1913 for land handling. These, and all other European flying-boat designs, had however been preceded by the American Glenn Curtiss who, on 12 January 1912, had made his first flight in a flying boat of his own design – the world's premier *successful* flying boat.

In 1913 Curtiss came to England with his latest design, where he first met John C Porte, test pilot then for the White & Thompson Company. Early in 1914 Porte travelled to the United States, there to join Curtiss as pilot of the projected Curtiss *America* flying boat being purpose-built for an intended trans-Atlantic attempted flight. The *America* incorporated several features, including an enclosed crew cabin, which in improved forms were to be standard items in most future designs, but its projected transocean flight was nullified by the outbreak of war in Europe on 4 August 1914. That same day John Porte sailed for England where he immediately enlisted in the RNAS. His first act on donning uniform was to inform the Director of the Admiralty Air Department, Murray Seuter, of the Curtiss flying boats. Seuter promptly ordered the purchase of two Curtiss machines, both of which were delivered in November 1914, and shortly after ordered 50 more to be built for the RNAS, all of which were delivered by late 1915. These formed the nucleus of the RNAS's contemporary flying-boat strength and were a foundation for Porte's own improved designs in the 'Felixstowe' class which later gave sterling service with the RNAS and RAF. One American first which seldom attracts

mention in aviation histories occurred on 1 January 1914, when Tony Jannus, an experienced pilot, took off from Tampa, Florida, in a biplane Benoist flying boat for a 22-mile over-water flight to St Petersburg, Florida, carrying a fare-paid passenger – the world's first scheduled passenger air service by airplane. Regrettably, Jannus's 'air line' lasted only a few weeks, being economically unsuccessful. The fare per passenger was a mere $5 – though this price increased if any passenger weighed more than 200 pounds (90.7 kg)!

The European war gave an inevitable impetus to the relatively fast development of flying boats and float-planes; the North Sea and eastern Atlantic waters now became a naval battleground and a hunting ground for Germany's submarine fleet preying on Allied mercantile shipping. While Germany at that stage had concentrated mainly on float versions of several excellent, proved land-plane designs for her marine units, France had already expressed official interest in flying boats for the protection of her coastal waters along the English Channel. The Franco-British Aviation Company (FBA) produced its first FBA design in mid-1912, a hybrid of previous French-designed flying boats. The FBA proved to have a good performance for its day, allied with pleasant handling characteristics, and was quickly ordered into production for the French Navy. The RNAS also showed interest in the FBA and bought one example in late 1912 – the first flying boat to enter British service use, incidentally – to be followed in subsequent years by healthy orders for further FBAs. Though a handful of these saw active service operations during 1914–16, the bulk of RNAS FBAs were employed as dual training machines throughout the war. In 1914, nevertheless, a majority of existing 'naval' aircraft were land-planes or twin-float airplanes; the latter in many cases were simply adapted land-planes with a change of undercarriage. It was a configuration largely progressed in Britain by the Short brothers, Horace, Eustace and Oswald – three very remarkable men who, by 1909, had formed the world's first aircraft manufacturing company in London. From their earliest examples – adapted copies of the Wright *Flyer* – the Short brothers' firm was to become recognized as the premier designer of flying boats and seaplanes during the next four decades.

Another British aircraft firm devoted from its outset to development of seagoing airplanes was the Supermarine Company, based at Southampton. Founded as a private company in 1912 by Noel Pemberton Billing, the title 'Supermarine' was registered in 1913, and the company set out to put into practice Billing's personal view that a true seagoing aircraft should be 'Not an airplane that will float but a boat that will fly.' Commencing with a remarkably streamlined little tractor flying boat, the PB1, which was exhibited at Olympia in 1914 (but never flew), Billing's company went on to produce a number of fairly advanced designs during World War I. This included the 1918 N.1B, a neat single-seat flying-boat biplane fighter – the first British fighter flying boat, though by no means the world's first such design – which was the progenitor of a long line of successful Supermarine seagoing aircraft during the next 15 years. In 1916 Billing entered Parliament and therefore sold out his interests in Supermarine, which henceforth came under the aegis of Hubert Scott-Paine, a noted marine engineer.

The bulk of British flying boats during the latter years of 1914–18 stemmed from the early Curtiss *America* design, but modified and greatly improved by John Porte who, as commander of the RNAS Station at Felixstowe, devoted himself tirelessly to his task of providing the RNAS with worthy seagoing aircraft. His ultimate design, a mammoth triple-winged boat titled *Felixstowe Fury*, appeared first in mid-1918. With wings spanning 123 feet, and powered by five 345-hp Rolls-Royce Eagle engines, the *Fury* was found to be easy to fly, even with an all-up weight exceeding 33,000 pounds, or – as on

one occasion – when lifting 24 passengers plus 5000 pounds of ballast. Though never flown operationally, it provided much data on large flying-boat design. The *Fury* was wrecked in 1919 and its creator, John Porte, died in October 1919 of pulmonary tuberculosis. Parallel with Porte's efforts, German designer Claud Dornier had commenced construction of a huge biplane flying boat, the Rs I, at Zeppelin's Friedrichshafen works in January 1915. In October of that same year the Rs I was launched, but was wrecked before official flight trials began. The lessons learned from its construction were then incorporated in Dornier's second machine, the Rs II, construction of which began in December 1915. Though having a pair of small lower wings, the Rs II was in essence a massive monoplane structure affixed to a boat hull 'fuselage.' Power came from three 240-hp Maybach Mb IV engines, offering a top speed of some 80 mph, and the main wing of the aircraft spanned a total of almost 109 feet.

Right: RAF maintenance crews learning the skills of mooring and anchoring a Southampton at Calshot. This particular machine, S1121, was the last wood-hull variant, and crashed on 17 October 1933, killing two of its crew.
Below: One of the RAF's sturdiest 'sea-boot warriors' of the interwar years was the Supermarine Southampton, known to its crews as 'Old Faithful.' Entering service in 1925, the type remained in first-line use until 1936. This example, K2965, belonged to 201 Squadron, based at Calshot.

Above: Blackburn Iris, N185, settles on its landing run at Felixstowe. First flown in 1926, the Iris and its development, the Perth, saw limited RAF service until 1937.

Right: Designed for the Mediterranean legs of Imperial Airways' England-to-India routes, the Short S.17 Kent first flew in 1931. Only three examples were built, named Scipio, Sylvanus, and the machine pictured here, Satyrus (G-ABFC), the latter surviving until 1938 before being scrapped.

Below: On the 'step.' Short Singapore III of 209 Squadron about to become airborne. Introduced to squadron service in 1935, the Singapore remained in use with the RAF until 1941, and with the RNZAF until 1945.

The Rs II first flew on 30 June 1918 and, after satisfactory flight trials, was dismantled and cannibalized to provide spare parts for a further, monoplane development. None of Dornier's flying boats saw active service during the war, but the accumulated experience of what had been virtually an unrestricted four years' 'research' program found successful outlets in several Dornier designs of the 1920s and 1930s.

On the operational aspect of the war, Germany was well served for maritime aircraft by the firms of Brandenburg and Friedrichshafen. The former firm's chief designer was Ernst Heinkel – later to be prominently associated with the Nazi Luftwaffe's machines of the 1930s and 1940s – whose W 12 biplane two-seater proved to be an excellent reply to the RNAS's heavily-armed Felixstowe flying boats of 1917–18. Of the many successful Friedrichshafen types to see operational service, the F.33 variants were undoubtedly the most useful. Mainly designed for patrols and reconnaissance in coastal waters, F.33s were often engaged in combat with the RNAS; individual machines, such as F.33e,841 Wölfchen, were carried aboard the German auxiliary cruiser Wolf, and during an extended 'cruise' from November 1916 to February 1918 in both the Pacific and Indian Oceans, participated in nearly all its parent ship's many successes against Allied shipping. Most German aircraft firms produced occasional 'marine' versions of their standard land-planes throughout the war, including the Gotha WD series of medium and giant seaplanes. The well-known fighter designers, Albatros, manufactured their W4 single-seat fighter seaplane which saw wide use during 1916–17.

The myriad problems of adapting the airplane to a maritime use were common to all nations' designers, and each resolved these in his own fashion. Yet by the close of the 1914–18 war the flying boat and float-plane – the two prime types of seagoing airplanes – were firmly established as viable modes of aerial transport. With the coming of peace thoughts turned logically to the possibilities of using such aircraft for commerce and communication. The advantages of a flying boat included the simple fact that it needed few facilities for normal flying operations, that is, it required no airdrome or lengthy runways from which to fly. Any reasonably clear stretch of water would suffice, and with the bulk of the earth's surface comprising water the range of operations seemed restricted only by the technical capability of aircraft engines and fuel capacity. Britain, with her global empire, was especially aware of such an application. The dream was of an aerial-linked 'all-red' route – the allusion being to all pre-1939 maps of the world which (in Britain) showed all countries within the British Empire in a red coloring. Land-based airplanes had yet to attain any wholly reliable technical status for such a global use, and in any case airdromes en route to any overseas territory were then nonexistent. The other alternative – the rigid airship – was considered feasible, at least by a section of the aeronautical fraternity, but had yet to demonstrate its true practicality. The flying boat, however, needed only simple harbor facilities for refuelling, pick-up of passengers or freight, and little else. The oceans were its airfields – at least, in theory.

In America the pioneer of flying boats, Glenn Curtiss, had pursued his research and experimentation throughout the war, and in 1918 produced a large three-engined boat, with wings spanning 126 feet – the NC1, or Navy Curtiss. Tests quickly demonstrated a need for a fourth engine, and the NC1's stablemates, NC2, NC3 and NC4, were thus powered. Intended originally for active service in Europe, the cessation of hostilities nullified a projected trans-Atlantic flight by NC1, piloted by Commander R E Byrd, USN, but postwar preparations for such a venture commenced in February 1919. With its cruising range of 1470 miles, the NC was clearly unable to contemplate a nonstop flight to Europe, and accordingly the proposed route was via the Azores to Lisbon, then England.

On 8 May 1919 three of the giant aircraft, NC1, NC3 and NC4, left Long Island, New York, on the first stage of their journey to Newfoundland. After delays due to weather and unserviceabilities, the trio finally took off for the Azores on 16 May. En route NC1 was forced to alight, 100 miles short of its objective, and hours later was abandoned; NC3 also landed on the ocean, was damaged, then taxied 200 miles in heavy seas before finally reaching Sao Miguel Island. NC4, piloted by Lieutenant-Commander A C Read and a five-man crew, reached the Azores safely and, once the local weather conditions permitted, took off on 27 May for Lisbon and reached his goal nearly 10 hours later. Four days later, to an ecstatic reception, Read landed NC4 in Plymouth Sound, having flown a total distance of 4320 miles in 53 hours and 58 minutes – the first-ever trans-Atlantic aerial crossing by any form of airplane. The following month saw two British airmen, John Alcock and Arthur Whitten-Brown, cross the Atlantic from Newfoundland to Eire nonstop in a Vickers Vimy.

In the following 10 years a number of attempts were made to emulate Read, Alcock and Brown in 'conquering the Atlantic.' Notably the successful first crossing of the South Atlantic was made by two Portuguese airmen, Senors Cabral and Coutinho, in a specially modified two-seat Fairey IIID float-plane named *Lusitania*, which took off from Lisbon on 30 March 1922 and eventually arrived in Rio de Janeiro on 17 June. The majority of such projects were, however – and perhaps somewhat illogically – undertaken by carefully modified land-planes, with or on occasion without wheeled undercarriages. Within the postwar Royal Air Force development of the pure flying boat was progressed steadily during the 1920s and early 1930s; such a design offered apparently limitless range for the RAF's prime overseas task of air-policing Britain's far-flung Empire. Allied to such a role was the more esoteric task of protection of Britain's mercantile fleet – the lifelines upon which an island kingdom depended for its existence – apart from the relatively minor assistance and adjunct duties with the Royal Navy. Foremost among flying-boat manufacturers and

designers in England were the Short brothers' firm at Rochester, but they were closely rivalled by both Supermarine and Vickers in flying-boat designs. Britain's aircraft industry then was still largely a matter of private enterprise in a highly competitive market, with only sparing support or encouragement from officialdom; thus a wide proliferation of aircraft types were built and offered to potential customers – albeit many of these projected flying boats having little to recommend them in terms of lengthy reliability.

During the immediate post-1918 years the RAF was content to continue using wartime designs such as the Felixstowe F3 and F5 flying boats. In 1925 the service received its first examples of a postwar design, the Supermarine Southampton, when No. 480 CR Flight at Calshot took delivery of a Southampton I on 25 August. Its roots lay in a civil flying boat, the Supermarine Swan, designed by R J Mitchell who in later years was responsible for the design of the legendary Spitfire fighter. Wooden-hulled, the Mk I Southampton began to be replaced two years later by an improved, metal-hulled Mk II version. On 17 October 1927 four RAF Southamptons under the overall command of Group Captain H M Cave-Brown-Cave, DSO, DFC, set out from Plymouth on the first leg of an astounding semi-global formation flight to Singapore. Known collectively as the

Far East Flight, this quartet of Southamptons was attempting a duration flight far beyond the capacity of any flying boat hitherto. The proposed route included vast stretches of ocean and land unknown to air crews of the time, while the problems of navigation, durability and seaworthiness of the aircraft had yet to be tested under such extreme conditions. During the following four months the Far East Flight completed flights to Singapore, Australia and around the China Sea – an overall distance of more than 24,000 miles without serious mishap and, with very minor exceptions, strictly on schedule. Their achievements were heralded by the world's press in superlatives and one newspaper called it 'The greatest flight in history.'

After some 10 years' faithful service the Southampton was phased out of RAF use, to be replaced by a succession of biplane flying boats until the eventual arrival of metal monoplane designs. Chief among the multiplane boats in RAF use thereafter were the Short Singapore, Blackburn Iris and Perth, Saro London and Supermarine Stranraer. None were manufactured in any great quantity, yet all provided vital links with the later, sleek monoplane boats, and indeed several Londons, Singapores, Stranraers and other biplanes were to see active service during the early years of World War II.

In America during the 1920s and early 1930s the chief exponent of the flying boat was Glenn Curtiss, who continued to produce a number of designs for US naval and civilian use. With rare exceptions the bulk of other American maritime aircraft were float-planes and/or float-amphibians, a form of seagoing design undertaken from as early as 1915 by such firms as Boeing, Loening and Douglas. Intensive research by the Curtiss firm also resulted in several high-speed biplane float-planes intended to compete in the international Schneider Trophy and other speed races of the period, but concentration on flying-boat designs by such manufacturers, and others such as Martin and Consolidated, did not figure largely until the advent of the monoplane in commercial and service aviation. The advantages of the float-plane were self-evident where flying involved covering territories which included vast stretches of rivers or lakes, and the adaptability of almost any land-plane design to a mere exchange of its undercarriage for twin floats was exploited by all nations throughout the twixt-wars period of aviation. By the mid-1930s, however, the all-metal monoplane flying boat was superseding existing bi-planes, and the majestic sight of 'boats that flew' with super-structures vaguely resembling the canvas-rigged schooners of romantic history gradually became a rare sight in the skies.

Right: **Supermarine Stranraers display their skills in tight formation flying. Stranraers saw wide service with the RAF and RCAF until at least 1943.**
Below: **Slipping the boat – a 201 Squadron Saro London, K5257, is put into the water at Calshot. Londons continued on first-line duties with the RAF until 1941 and with the RCAF thereafter.**

Bell-Bottoms

While the early decades of maritime aviation history tend to be apparently dominated by the large flying boat – the type of aircraft succinctly defined by Pemberton Billing as '. . . a boat that will fly' – the urge and indeed necessity for applying the airplane to a divergency of purely naval functions resulted in a wide variety of custom-built 'bell-bottomed' aircraft designs during the main biplane era. Such seaplanes can be broadly categorized in two main streams of designs: the float-under-carriage for use *on* water, and the more usual wheeled-undercarriage types for use aboard aircraft carriers and similarly adapted vessels. There was, of course, a third variation, a compromise – the amphibian design. In particular, carrierborne aircraft and their crews created a form of aerial weaponry which was to have a highly significant effect on the war of 1939–45 and on general strategic thinking in later years.

The beginnings of maritime aviation, described in the last chapter, led inevitably to widespread employment of seaplanes and flying boats throughout World War I. Yet perhaps the most significant development was the initial trials and operational use of the torpedo-carrying seaplane, a weapon which would alter many centuries of entrenched naval thinking. The pioneering experiments with aircraft carrying torpedoes commenced in 1911, when an Italian, Captain Guidoni, claimed to have successfully air-launched a torpedo from a Farman aircraft – a claim of dubious confirmation. Certainly, the first British (and probably the world's) torpedo drop was carried out in the Solent by Squadron Commander A Longmore, RN, on 28 July 1914. Flying a Short Folder float-plane, No. 121, from RNAS Station Calshot, Longmore successfully launched a 14-inch Mk X torpedo. Longmore's feat was, in reality, more a proving flight

Left: The Wight Navyplane, No. 128 at Calshot, 1914, with Squadron Commander (later, Sir Arthur) Longmore in its cockpit.
Below: Eugene Ely making the first landing, at 40 mph, on the cruiser *Pennsylvania* in a Curtiss biplane on 18 January 1911. Eager interest by the ship's crew is self evident.

Left: An RNAS Sopwith Pup, having been floated out to its parent ship by pontoons, about to be hoisted aboard.
Right: Beaching a Friedrichshafen FF33 variant required old-fashioned muscle power.
Below right: Fairey Hamble *Baby* scout being 'slipped' for an air test.

than any distinct armament experiment, illustrating that even the contemporary, underpowered aircraft could lift such a heavy weapon.

There is no doubt whatsoever about the first-ever actual attack attended with success for the airborne torpedo. This took place on 12 August 1915 from a Short 184 float-plane, No. 842, piloted by Lieutenant C H K Edmonds, RN. As one of the complement of the ship *Ben-my-Chree* in Mediterranean waters, Edmonds set out at dawn that day seeking enemy shipping reported in the approaches to the Sea of Marmora, and eventually sighted a small group of vessels lying just west of Injeh Burnu. Selecting a large steamer as his target, Edmonds flew in at 15 feet height and, at 800 yards' range, launched his torpedo, which hit the ship on the starboard side just below the mainmast area. The steamer settled by the stern, and Edmonds duly returned to Xeros. Unknown to him at the time, his target had in fact been torpedoed and shelled by the British submarine E14 some four days previously; nevertheless, the portent of Edmonds' feat was not lost on the naval hierarchy. Five days later Edmonds, again in No. 842, torpedoed another enemy ship which later sank; his companion on this occasion, Flight Lieutenant G B Dacre, though forced to alight due to a fractious engine, coolly taxied within range of another ship, launched his torpedo, and sank it into the side of a large tug.

The wider application of aviation for naval purposes, the use of aircraft aboard seagoing vessels, can be said to have been envisaged with astonishing accuracy as early as 1909. It was then that the renowned French inventor Clement Ader, in his publication *L'Aviation Militaire*, described a ship having a flat, unobstructed decking, with below-deck housing reached by mechanical lift-platforms, and airplanes with folding wings for such accommodation – the first practical prescience of the modern aircraft carrier. Though this prevision was not to achieve actual form for another nine years, in the interim the Royal Navy began successful trials of aircraft being launched from ships. As related, the first takeoff (and landing back) from a naval vessel was accomplished by the American Eugene B Ely in November 1910; the bulk of pioneering trials thereafter were undertaken by Britain's naval pilots. Chief among these in the years 1912–18 was Charles Rumney Samson, whose takeoffs from temporary wood 'runways' mounted over the fo'c's'le of standard naval ships in 1912 presaged a series of increasingly successful trials in the following years. Perhaps the most significant of these took place on 7 May 1913 when a Caudron amphibian (No. 55) was flown off a small deck mounted on the forward superstructure of HMS *Hermes*; it was the first takeoff with a *wheeled* undercarriage.

By 1914 several British ships were being converted into seaplane carriers, but the first to have a flying-off deck incorporated as a permanent fitment appeared in 1915, when the

18,000 tons *Campania* was commissioned for RN service on 17 April 1915, commanded by Captain O Swann, RN. The *Campania*'s first successful takeoff occurred on 6 August when Flight Lieutenant W L Welsh took off in Sopwith Schneider No. 1559, fitted with a jettisonable wheeled dolly. Then on 3 November 1915 Flight Lieutenant F Fowler made an historic takeoff from the forward deck of HMS *Vindex* in a normally wheeled single-seat Bristol Scout C (No. 1255) – the first occasion on which a military aircraft with wheeled undercarriage had flown in wartime from a ship specifically fitted for such a purpose. Such a feat served to encourage a continuing series of both takeoff and landing-on experimentation for aircraft with wheel undercarriages; in early 1916 Commodore Murray Seuter, RN, a devotee of naval aviation, ordered the prototype of an airplane eventually to become the Sopwith Cuckoo – the first torpedo airplane ever designed to operate from an aircraft carrier. By mid-1917 many normal RN ships were being modified to carry a small flying-off platform structure forward, often mounted above forward gun batteries. In this way, at least such ships could be provided with their own scouts for reconnaissance and ship's defense roles.

In July 1917 HMS *Furious* officially joined the Fleet; she was originally a battle cruiser, but was modified during construction to incorporate a 228-foot flying deck forward. On 2 August Squadron Commander E H Dunning successfully landed a single-seat Sopwith Type 9901 on *Furious*'s deck – an historic first – but lost his life only days later on a similar trial landing. Nevertheless, *Furious* was to be the 'host' to a naval operation historical event the following year when, on 19 July 1918, seven Sopwith 2F.1 Camels flew from its deck and bombed German airship sheds at Tondern, destroying two Zeppelins housed therein (L.54 and L.60). It was the world's first aircraft-carrier air strike – true naval air power had been blooded. And in October 1918 HMS *Argus*, the first full, flush-deck aircraft carrier to enter service, received the first full squadron, No. 185, of carrierborne torpedo-carrying aircraft, Sopwith Cuckoos. The means, methods and appropriate weaponry for naval air warfare were now in a complete, if still embryo, form – a strike force able to operate virtually anywhere.

The coming of peace diluted further naval experimentation, though carrier techniques continued to improve modestly during the post-bellum years, while the slowly recognized need for airplanes specifically designed for naval use resulted in a steadily expanding proliferation of fresh designs from aircraft manufacturers. If such aircraft were, ostensibly, produced solely with a naval employment uppermost in the designers' minds, a great majority of them possessed an uncannily similar characteristic – acute ugliness in appearance. While this is a quality which can also be associated with many other forms of military aircraft, it seemed to be almost a prerequisite for naval aircraft during the 1920s and early 1930s. If one considers objectively the peculiar needs of any carrierborne airplane, there seems no weighty reason why 'bell-bottomed' aircraft *should* have been any less aesthetically pleasing than any other form of military role. Folding wings were an obvious advantage for parking aircraft in the highly limited space available on any fighting ship, and the eventual necessity for the addition of arrester hook gear under the fuselages became a recognized excrescence. For torpedo aircraft the undercarriage of biplanes was necessarily divided to accommodate the 'fish' – though in more modern eras such weapons have come to be stowed in bomb bays in the same manner as any other explosive store.

Left: The original Short 184, viewed at its makers' works at Rochester, Kent, complete with 14-inch torpedo slung between its undercarriage floats, March 1915. In this state it had only single-acting ailerons.
Below left: Sopwith 2F.1, N6603, taking off from the forward 'deck' of HMS *Pegasus*, 1918.
Right: Albatros W4 float-fighters saw operational service from 1916 to 1917, a development of the land-based Albatros D.1 Scout with similar twin-gun armament.

Initially too, designers tended toward the (mistaken) theory that all aircraft operating from a carrier deck required relatively low performance capabilities, that is, ultra-low speeds for landing-on, and steady but by no means excessive power for takeoffs. In World War II such theories were abruptly shattered.

In Britain if the adolescent Royal Air Force suffered almost two decades of unabated opposition and miserly financial budgeting, the naval air arm – titled Fleet Air Arm from April 1924 – was an even more poverty-stricken cousin. Still under the aegis of RAF control and general financial control, the FAA was not to come completely under Admiralty administration until 1937. The failure of the RAF and Admiralty to nurture Britain's naval air arm may be judged by the simple fact that at the outbreak of war in 1939, the FAA could barely boast of 20 squadrons comprising a total of some 340 aircraft of all types. Yet, paradoxically, the two aircraft carriers inherited from 1918 – *Furious* and *Argus* – were supplemented by no less than five new aircraft carriers by World War II; *Eagle* (1922), *Hermes* (1923), *Glorious* & *Courageous* (1928) and *Ark Royal* (1938). Deck-arresting gear for aircraft being retrieved continued in experimental forms until, in 1933, the basic system for transverse arrester wires hooked to friction brake-drums with resetting mechanisms was perfected – the nucleus of today's deck systems. One other method of launching aircraft from seagoing ships was catapulting, a method first tried in 1917 but not perfected until late 1925 in the FAA. Such a method enabled 'noncarriers' – for example, battleships, cruisers et al – to carry their own single or pair of 'spotter' aircraft primarily for reconnaissance and long-range direction of the ship's guns.

Though the RAF clung reluctantly to biplanes for its front-line equipment throughout most of the interwar years, at least it began to plan well ahead for replacement of such outmoded designs from the early 1930s and, indeed, managed to introduce many of these into squadron service by 1939, albeit in relatively small numbers. The Fleet Air Arm, however, lacked any such forward planning at Admiralty levels, resulting in a first-line strength comprised – with the one exception of the Blackburn Skua dive-bomber monoplane – entirely of biplanes at the outbreak of war with Germany. From 1918 to 1939 the main stream of FAA operational aircraft were mainly the products of two British aircraft manufacturers: Blackburn and Fairey. Neither firm in those years was particularly noted for producing beautiful airplanes in the aesthetic sense, but both applied their considerable experience to fulfilling the official specifications issued for naval aircraft. From Blackburn's designers flowed a succession of ponderous, ugly-snouted, all-purpose two- and three-seat biplanes – the Dart, Blackburn, Ripon, Baffin and Shark – all torpedo-carrying bombers in keeping with the naval faith in the airborne torpedo as a principal strike weapon. From the Fairey concern came the long line of Mk III variants, Seal, diminutive and much-beloved Flycatcher fighter, and, of course, the legendary 'Stringbag' or Swordfish and Albacore of World War II fame. Not until the early 1930s did the FAA begin to receive more pleasant-looking (and more efficient) aircraft from the Hawker firm, when adapted variants of its classic Hart bomber and Fury fighter emerged as the Hawker Osprey and Nimrod respectively.

While the Fairey Swordfish and its ostensible successor, the Albacore, achieved lasting niches in maritime aerial warfare during the 1939–45 war, a lesser-known stablemate, the Fairey Seafox, also made its brief but memorable contribution to the biplanes' fighting record. Designed specifically as a light recce, catapult two-seater for use aboard Royal Navy ships of the line, the Seafox will always be associated with the first notable naval victory of 1939. During the Battle of the River Plate, when three cruisers forced the German battleship *Admiral Graf Spee* to seek shelter in Montevideo port, a Seafox from HMS *Ajax*, piloted by Lieutenant E D G Lewin, maintained a continuous 'spotting' role for its parent ship's guns and also strafed the German ship's decks. Then on 17 December its crew were overhead when the *Graf Spee* moved out of harbor and was scuttled by explosives. Its pilot was later decorated – the first FAA officer so honored during World War II.

While Britain's Royal Navy was responsible for virtually all pioneering experimentation and application of maritime aerial warfare during 1912–18, it was by no means the only national navy to become interested in this new branch of aviation. In the United States the Navy Department appointed an officer, Captain W I Chambers, USN, to deal with all aspects of aviation with effect from September 1910. For the following three years Chambers created the departmental framework from which US naval air power was to evolve, and he was also responsible for selecting the designer, Glenn Curtiss, to build the first pair of US Navy airplanes. The first of these was the Curtiss A-1 Triad which first flew in July 1911. By then two USN officers (T G Ellyson and J Rodgers) had already completed pilot training. By April 1914 the tiny US Navy aviation formation was able to commence reconnaissance duties for the Fleet during the US-Mexican crisis. On 1 July 1915 an Office of Naval Aeronautics came into being, and within a year a Naval Flying Corps (sic) was paper-established for a strength of 150 officers and 350 enlisted men. On 6 April 1917, the day the United States officially entered the European war, the NFC possessed 54 aircraft plus 48 qualified or trainee pilots. Its expansion during the next 20 months was dramatic; by the Armistice of November 1918 the NFC could count 2107 airplanes and 15 airships of the dirigible type, and a manning strength of 6716 officers and 30,693 enlisted men. A further 282 officers and 2180 enlisted men belonged to the US Marine Corps.

Although the Bureau of Aeronautics (BuAer) was created on 10 August 1921 to be responsible for all naval aviation affairs, a bitter feud ensued between the Army and the Navy – parallelling the interservice battling over the RAF in Britain – over control in policy, strategy and indeed equipment for the various aviation services. Such rivalry virtually ceased in 1931 when the Pratt-MacArthur agreement ratified the naval air force as an element of the Fleet, though Marine Aviation remained under the aegis of the USMC. By then naval aircraft strength – inevitably drastically pruned in the immediate post-1918 period – was slowly building to more than 1000. Within the limitations imposed by the Washington Treaty of February 1922, the United

States commissioned its first aircraft carrier, the USS *Langley* – a converted collier originally named *Jupiter* – in September 1922. Three years later she embarked the first squadron of regular US Navy aircraft. It might be noted here that only three months after the USS *Langley* entered service Japan commissioned its first aircraft carrier, the *Hosho*, with a 21-aircraft complement.

The gradual development of US naval air strength in the 1920s and early 1930s ran along roughly parallel lines with other nations' equivalent forces. Aircraft specifically designed for maritime use proliferated from the many established aircraft manufacturers throughout America, particularly such firms as Curtiss, Douglas and Martin, with the long-established Boeing firm, soon becoming contenders for official contracts. In addition the BuAer awarded contracts to the Naval Aircraft Factory, which produced the highly functional NAF TS-1 fighter in early 1922 – the first US carrier-based airplane specifically designed for that purpose. Like many of its successors, the TS-1 could interchange its wheel undercarriage for a standard twin-float arrangement. Progression of the torpedo bomber received reasonably high priority from 1918; one of the first and one of the US Navy's most successful designs was the Douglas DT of 1921, the company's first military airplane. Serving from 1922–26, in common with most of the world's naval aircraft, the DT

came to be used in a variety of roles. The design selected as eventual replacement for the DT was Curtiss's first torpedo bomber, the CS-1, which entered service in 1924. Built also under contract by the Martin company, the experience gained by this company led to an improved design, the Martin T3M-1, which entered service in 1926 and eventually became standard equipment of all naval torpedo squadrons. Improved variants continued in service until later replacement by such metal monoplanes as the Douglas TBD-1 which spelled the demise of the biplane torpedo bomber in USN use.

Apart from torpedo work, US naval aircraft also concentrated on development of Fleet observation designs, dive-bombing – a

Right: The Fairey III series of land- and float-planes gave long, doughty service throughout the 1920s and early 1930s; this IIID variant, N9633, is one of RAF Calshot's brood of maritime aircraft.
Below: Exemplifying the general ugliness of most 'naval' aircraft of its era, the Blackburn *Blackburn* (S1048 here) with its multistrutted structure was an all-purpose design.
Bottom right: By 1918 the value of the airborne torpedo had been well established in most air services. Sopwith Cuckoo, N6966, is illustrated, dropping its 'fish' on a trial drop, 1918.

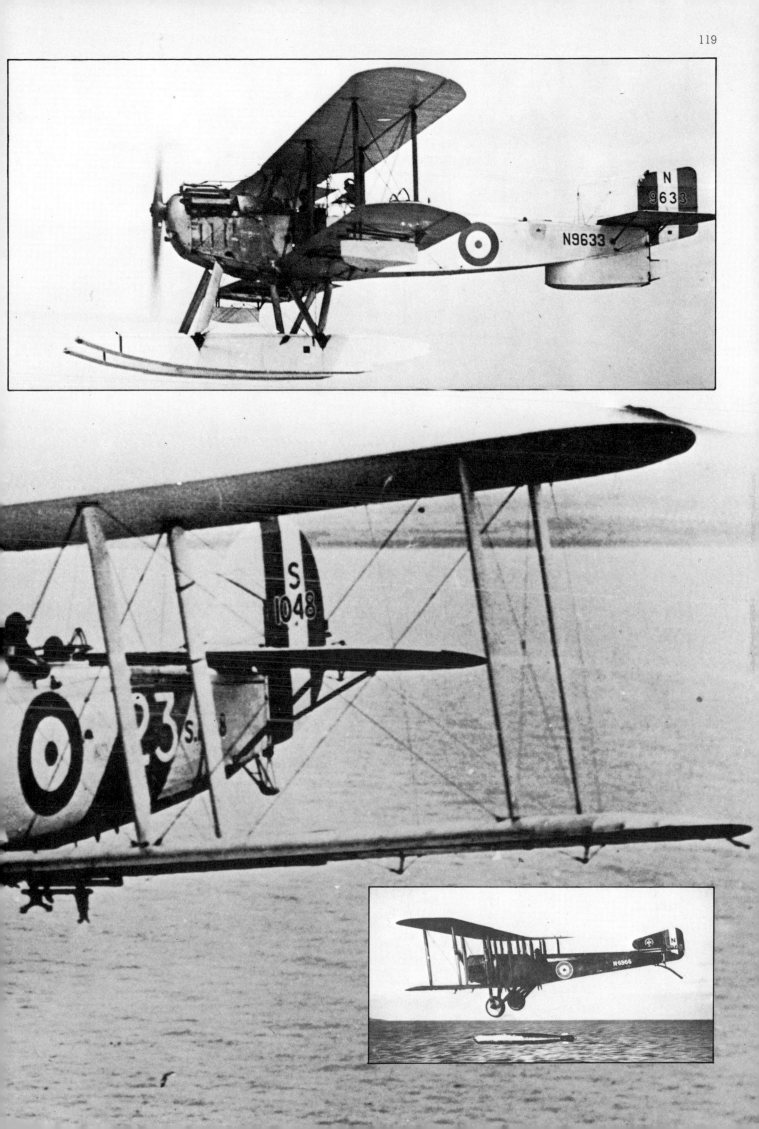

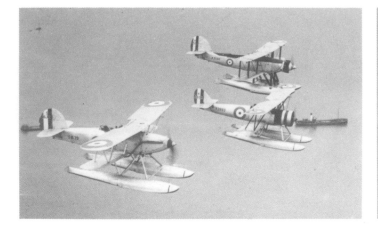

Above: Three different designs in use with the Calshot Seaplane Training Squadron in 1935: Hawker Osprey, S1679; Avro Sea Tutor, K2893; and Fairey Seal, K3530.
Above right: German float-recce Arado Ar 95A-1.
Opposite, top left: The American Grumman J2F-6 *Duck* amphibian first appeared in its original form in 1933, but continued to be built up to 1942, and served throughout World War II in its various versions.
Opposite, top right: A two-seat float reconnaissance biplane, a Heinkel He 60 B-3, used by the Luftwaffe in the late 1930s.
Right: The emergent Nazi Luftwaffe invested in float variants of their standard fighters in the mid-1930s, in this case a 'bell-bottomed' Heinkel He 51B of Coastal Fighter Gruppe 136.

vogue which received equal attention later by the embryo Luftwaffe – and, naturally, naval fighters. In this last category the US Navy and the USMC were able to benefit greatly from the spin-off from the various excellent fighter types being produced for the US Army's air arm; such designs as the Boeing FBs, Curtiss Hawks, and, later, the tubby Grumman products were to become almost an exclusive naval aircraft series. Indeed, the Grumman XFF-1 two-seat fighter was the first US Navy fighter to incorporate a retractable undercarriage, and led to the famous single-seat F2F and F3F fighters which began first-line service in 1935. It fell to the Grumman F3F-3 variant to become the last biplane fighter to be ordered for any US armed service, when 27 examples were ordered for the Navy in June 1938. Mention should be made of two Curtiss designs which achieved particular niches in USN history; the Curtiss SOC Seagull, a two-seat observation biplane which was the last Curtiss biplane to be used by the USN and could proudly claim to have flown on first-line duties throughout World War II; and the Curtiss SBC Helldiver, the last combat biplane produced in America.

In Germany, despite the total restriction on any form of military air service or aircraft construction or design in the vengeful Versailles Treaty, the resurrection of a German air force began in total secrecy in the early 1920s. In its original conception the intended German air force was to be independent of army or navy overall control. Until Hitler's blatant revelation of the Luftwaffe's existence in 1935 the general aircraft types used to train the embryo air service were a wide mixture of biplanes and monoplanes. That year saw German designers leapfrog into the monoplane era, with the first flight testing of several prototypes which presaged many of the standard Luftwaffe operational airplanes used throughout 1939–45. The bulk of planning for Germany's future aerial might was aimed toward land-based aircraft, for cooperation with the army; naval aviation retained a relatively minor role. Germany's first aircraft carrier, *Graf Zeppelin*, was not launched until December 1938, and was destined never to see active operations throughout World War II. Thus, the only roles envisaged for naval aircraft were those of coastal defense and reconnaissance, the latter to include catapult aircraft borne on individual

ships of the line. The early years saw the naval coastal units equipped with several biplane types, notably the various Heinkel designs then in wide use in various forms. These were soon replaced by more modern monoplane airplanes. One advantage for the Luftwaffe, which was almost built from scratch in the early 1930s, was the opportunity to benefit from other air forces' development toward truly modern aircraft lines of progression.

The same relatively rapid conversion to all-monoplane naval air services was evident in the growth of most nations by the early 1930s. The faithful biplane, though usually beloved by its crews, was an anachronism in the context of modern aerial warfare as the airplane entered its fourth decade of existence. In the case of naval aircraft, with the peculiar requirements of their various roles, all-metal monoplanes offered greater range, far better performances and perhaps more reliable endurance in the necessary rough and tumble of all naval operations. With rare, and often outstanding individual exceptions, the 'bell-bottomed' biplane had died a natural evolutionary death by the late 1930s. Nevertheless, it had paved the way splendidly for a form of warfare which was to be decisive during the global conflict of 1939–45.

Right: A Grumman J2F is being hoisted out, with a crewman providing human 'balance' on its starboard wing-tip.
Below: The Curtiss SOC Seagull was the last Curtiss-designed biplane in operational use with the US Navy. This SOC-1 belonged to VCS-14, pictured on 24 February 1937. The Seagull, like most float aircraft could be easily converted to a wheeled undercarriage. They remained in USN service until 1944.

Fighter Heyday

The single-seat airplane commenced its operational role during World War I as a 'scout,' the aerial equivalent of the traditional cavalry 'point' riding ahead of his squadron, seeking enemy dispositions and guiding the path forward of his main troop. As such it was merely an adjunct of the early military airplane's *raison d'etre* of reconnaissance. By 1916, however, the single-seat airplane had come to be regarded as an offensive weapon

in its own right, a fighter in every sense of the word. In the years 1916–18 fighter aircraft and their crews, of all nations, carved out a new form of warfare and firmly established the fighter as a distinct type of design indispensable to all future military air services. Inadvertently, perhaps, those formative years of the fighter-aircraft concept also gave birth to the continuing aura and charisma of the fighter ace; the steely eyed, highly individual hero of a thousand fiction books, articles and films. As in all legends, the ace cult had its base in fact. Throughout the first-ever aerial war, a host of fighter pilots achieved honor, fame, and too often, death for their prowess in the arena of the skies. The age-old concept of man-versus-man in single combat, with its overtones of chivalry and ultimate courage harped back to the (mainly) fictional aura of the medieval knights at tourney, jousting to the death in defense of honor and a code of high moral conduct.

In reality fighter combat during World War I, and indeed ever since, was an affair of kill or be killed; it was a swift, merciless clash in which each opponent sought to destroy each other by any means available. However, the ideal killing tactic taught in every air service was to get behind an enemy and shoot him in the back, preferably without even being seen by the victim. The term 'ace' originated with the romantic French press and came to be adopted by virtually all nations' aviation services, except the British – who never *officially* listed or described their high-scoring pilots thus – and was applied to any pilot

Top: An uncowled Curtiss P-3A Hawk of 1928 vintage.
Above: One of a long line of highly successful US Army fighters of the 1920s and 1930s was this Curtiss Hawk P-6.
Far left: The Thomas-Morse MB-3A was the first US Army pursuit aircraft design to be produced in quantity post-1918. Capable of a speed of 150 mph, it carried standard twin machine guns as offensive armament.

claiming at least five aerial combat victories in the Allied services, and 10 victories in the air forces of the Central Powers. Successful aces were lauded in almost all countries, heaped with awards, honors and privileges, and their deeds were widely broadcast to a hero-hungry civil population for propaganda purposes. Such plaudits increased in proportion to each man's mounting tally of victims – a grisly paradox of death in some of its more horrifying forms for the victim and public worship of the conqueror. In common with all war pilots, the fighter ace, despite his uncommon expertise and experience, was not immune to the hazards of his trade; death in combat claimed seven of the top 20 RFC/RAF aces, and six of Germany's *kanonen* in their 20 highest-scoring fighters. Entry to an aerial Valhalla was never restricted to the least-experienced tyro.

If the fighter pilots gained international acclaim, the aircraft in which they achieved such fame also acquired near-legendary status in the annals of military aviation. Of these, certain fighter designs of the 1916–18 period were in some respects outstanding for their designated role. On British squadrons the foremost single-seaters were the various aircraft to come from the Sopwith 'stable,' in particular the Sopwith Pup, Triplane, Camel and Dolphin. Of equal fame in 1917–18 was the Farnborough-designed SE5 and SE5a; while the long-established Bristol Company produced its two-seat Bristol F2b Fighter, a design later accorded the earned title of 'King of Two-seaters.' The Sopwith Camel was to gain the undisputed reputation of World War I's most destructive fighter – in *any* nation's air service – with a final war tally for its myriad pilots of almost 3000 claimed victories over opponents in the air. As such it has become synonymous with the 1914–18 aerial war, and deserves its fame. A rotary-engined single-seater of snub-nosed, pugnacious appearance, the Camel embodied powers of maneuverability which fitted it superbly for its task, and – significantly – was the first British fighter designed from the outset to incorporate twin synchronized machine guns fixed forward of the cockpit, firing along the line of flight through the propeller arc. Its immediate successor from the Sopwith factory, the Dolphin, also had this classic armament installation, but added two Lewis machine guns on an upper bar – a four-gun fighter in 1918! Its contemporary, the SE5a, compromised with armament of one fixed synchronized Vickers gun in the fuselage, and a hand-operated Lewis gun on an upper-wing slide rail mounting. Though less mercurial in maneuverability than the waspish Camel, the

sturdy SE5a, with its stationary engine, was rugged and a more 'solid' gun-platform; these were qualities which were well exploited by such outstanding fighters as Edward Mannock, VC, 'Jimmy' McCudden, VC, and the Canadian VC, 'Billy' Bishop.

In the French *escadrilles* the two main types of fighter used from 1916 to 1918 were the compact Nieuport 'Vee-Strut' sesqui-plane single-seaters and the more conventionally designed Spad S7 and S13 fighters. Both types were also flown extensively by British, Italian and Belgian services. The many variants of the delicate-looking little Nieuport Scout gave trojan service in 1916–17, and were the mounts of many leading Allied aces. The greatest exponent of the tiny silver Nieuport was the 20-year-old Nottingham boy, Albert Ball, VC, DSO, MC, who gained the bulk of his accredited victories from the cramped cockpit of a Nieuport. The rugged Spad, which in the main re-equipped Nieuports among French and Italian squadrons, offered more strength in the dive and, accordingly, a steadier gun-base for actual shooting. Its inherent strength of construction gave added confidence to its pilots, and it was used to great effect by the 1918 French and American fighter pilots.

Opposing such aircraft, the German *jagdstaffeln* were equipped with equally good fighter designs throughout the war. The most prominent fighter of the 1916–18 period was the bullet-nosed, shark-tailed Albatros D line of single-seaters, commencing with the twin-gun D.I of late 1916 and progressing through the D.II, D.III and D.V of later months. The D.I can be regarded in many ways as the true 'Father of fighters,' in that it first introduced the concept of twin forward-firing, fixed guns armament, combined with a stationary engine, near-streamlined outline of fuselage, and semimonocoque ply-skinned construction of body. On its introduction it outgunned and out-

Right: Developed from an original 1918 design, the Armstrong Whitworth Siskin fighter had a surprisingly long life in active Service flying; the last examples were still in RCAF squadron use as late as 1939. Here a formation of Siskin IIIas of 43 Squadron, RAF are seen practicing for an RAF Display.
Below: Bristol Bulldogs of 17 Squadron RAF get away in Vic formation. After entering RAF service in 1929, Bulldogs gave sterling service in several air forces for some 10 years, with one small batch in the Finnish Air Force actually seeing active combat in the 'Winter War' against the USSR during 1939.

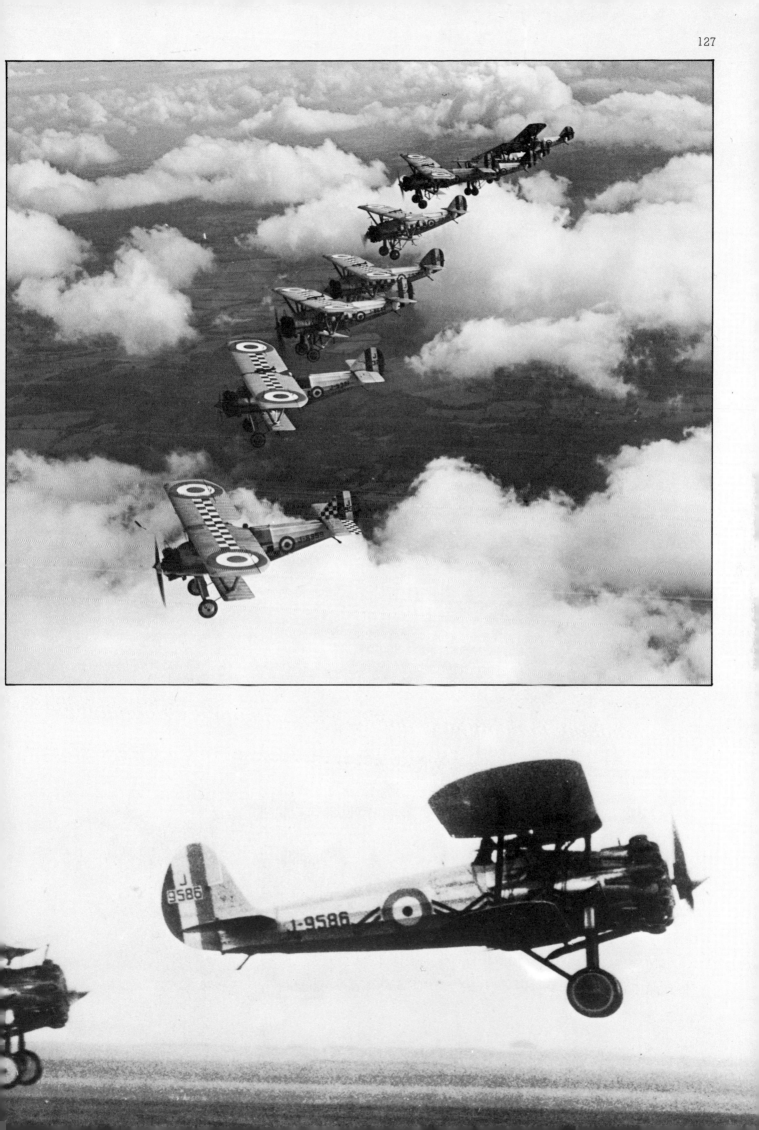

climbed every contemporary Allied opponent, giving German fighters several months of overt aerial supremacy over the Western Front. The basic needs for any fighter design – good maneuverability without loss of vital height, good climbing powers, and, if possible, high speed – had become recognized by all designers by 1916–17. One result on the German side was the notorious Fokker Dr1 Triplane, introduced initially to operations in August 1917 by Leutnant Werner Voss of *Jagdstaffel* 10, a unit within Manfred von Richthofen's *Jagdgeschwader* Nr 1, and within three weeks Voss had claimed some 21 victories in the little *dreidecker* (three-winger). From September 1917 until mid-1918 Fokker Dr1s were prominent among Germany's first-line units, but in April 1918 *Jagdgeschwader* Nr 1 received the first example of a new Fokker biplane, the D VII.

If the Fokker Dr1 triplane gained notoriety, mainly by its association with von Richthofen's Circus and other leading fighter units, the Fokker D VII outclassed the type in all departments and became the acknowledged best German fighter in general use of the war. Simple in design and construction, the D VII was said to be capable of turning even mediocre flyers into good combat pilots due to its excellent handling qualities and superlative performance range. The simplest tribute to the quality of the Fokker D VII was a now well-publicized paragraph of the November 1918 Armistice conditions, which specified the immediate surrender of all aircraft of the Fokker D VII type in prime condition, the only deliberate reference to a particular aircraft design in the document.

While the Fokkers and Albatros *jagdeinsitzers* (hunting one-seaters) formed the bulk of fighter equipment of the German services, a wide variety of secondary types were also flown in 'combat – notably the Pfalz D III and, in the earlier years, Halberstadt D fighters. By the closing months of the war, however, a few promising designs were filtering into combat units, including the Siemens-Schuckert D.III and D.IV rotary-

Probably the most famous of a long series of snub-nosed Boeing fighter designs, the F4B – in this view, an F4B-2, 8638 of VF-3 Squadron – first flew in May 1929, and entered USN service the same year. It remained in service until mid-1942.

engined biplanes. Sensitive in control, the SS Scouts gave substantial improvement over many existing contemporaries in rate of climb and maneuverability, features which led to many SS Scouts being sent to home defense units. Had the war continued for even a few more months, the SS Scouts and other fresh types would probably have supplemented the favored Fokker D VII as Germany's fighter spearhead. Such aircraft represented the tip of an iceberg in relation to an astonishing variety of

One of two Curtiss Hawks (F.11c) bought by the Luftwaffe for personal evaluation by Ernst Udet, who used them, in part, to pursue his faith in dive-bombing tactics.

experimental and tested fighters produced throughout the war by virtually every aircraft firm. Many of the latter helped to pioneer aspects of design and construction which became standard in several post-1918 fighter aircraft. Examples of this forward thinking were such machines as the Zeppelin-Lindau D.I biplane, designed by Claude Dornier in 1918, with its cantilever (that is, without interplane struts) wings and stressed-skin, all-metal fuselage – almost a compromise between the biplane configuration and the cleaner monoplane.

In the main, the other countries involved in the conflict – Austria, Italy, Belgium and America – tended to rely heavily on French, British and German designs with which to equip their respective fighter arms. Indeed, no American-designed aircraft, of *any* type, saw combat service prior to the Armistice. As the war drew to an uneasy peace, fresh designs of fighter were already reaching the combat squadrons within the RAF. One such was an intended successor to the doughty Camel, the Sopwith Snipe, which was introduced to the air war by 43 Squadron in late September 1918. Only two other units received Snipes in time to see any action in France, but in the following years the type equipped a number of RAF units. Another fighter with excellent potential, the Martinsyde F4 *Buzzard*, which was intended to equip no less than 13 RAF squadrons by mid-1919, arrived too late for war operations. The arrival of peace nullified this intention and the *Buzzard*, considered by many to have been the finest single-seat fighter then in existence, was never to equip even a single squadron. Indeed, the 1918 Armistice brought a near-halt to almost all immediate further development of the fighter in every aviation force, as each nation turned to the problems of resuming a peaceful existence and resurrecting trade and commercial life. Finance for purely military ventures was simply not available, while potential markets for any such new aircraft were minimal.

Existing air forces in the immediate post-bellum era were drastically reduced as a natural consequence of mass de-mobilization of millions of airmen, allied with a perfectly natural abhorrence by the civil populations of any form of war machinery. In Britain the infant Royal Air Force – at that moment the world's largest and first independent (of Army or Navy control) air force – was reduced to a tenth of its wartime strength in men and aircraft. It then had to begin a struggle destined to last two decades to retain not only its independence but its very existence, as both Army and Navy hierarchy fought tooth and nail to disperse the extant RAF between the two more senior services. Fortunately for future generations their efforts found little success, but the restrictions in governmental financial budget for the peacetime RAF left little to spare for normal progression in aircraft design. Hence, for several years the standard RAF fighter was the wartime Snipe. Of the other major nations, France's aviation field stagnated for a decade, and only began to progress in the 1930s. Germany, shackled by unrealistically harsh, punitive restrictions on all aspects of aviation in the Versailles Treaty, was forbidden to develop military aircraft and was forced to proceed rebuilding its air services in deepest secrecy outside the borders of Germany. In the United States the tardy, if massive, aircraft production programs of 1918 were almost totally cancelled at the Armistice, and the US Air Service, an adjunct still of the US Signal Corps, suffered the same deprivation of funds and enthusiasm encountered by the RAF, with a parallel lull in development of fresh designs. Of course, all the wartime air forces already held huge stocks of 1918–19 produced aircraft, far more than they had men or facilities with which to cope. In the United States, many pursuit (that is, fighter) squadrons made good use of wartime SE5as, Fokker D VIIs and other obsolete fighters for several years in the 1920s.

The general pattern of development of the fighter during the

Heinkel He 51B-1s of I Gruppe, *Jagdgeschwader* 134, *Horst Wessel* at Werl in 1936.

first post-1918 decade was remarkably similar in most existing air services. The apparently rapid progress in airplane design throughout 1914–18 had, in fact, only applied in the main to better engines, better methods of construction and improvement in a variety of minor details. Little had been accomplished, relatively, in the field of pure armament, despite the prime requirement of any fighter to be basically a 'flying gun-platform.' The twin-gun installation pioneered by the 1916 Albatros D.I in Germany and Sopwith Camel in Britain was accepted as adequate for all 1920s' fighters, and indeed continued to be so well into the 1930s in most cases. Yet much time and effort was expended on improving aircraft speeds and general performance ranges, albeit only in small stages, thereby in essence leaving gun performance lagging badly behind in efficiency. Ammunition of wartime vintage, combined with machine guns with rates of fire suited to 1918 fighter speeds, were palpably unsuited to aircraft capable of speeds 50 percent faster than their predecessors. Consequently target acquisition (the few seconds in which an enemy aircraft remained within an attacker's sights) left any attacker with a lesser weight of bullets actually hitting his target. The obvious solution was to introduce completely new guns, but design, testing and proving any new machine gun or cannon might take up to 10 years under con-

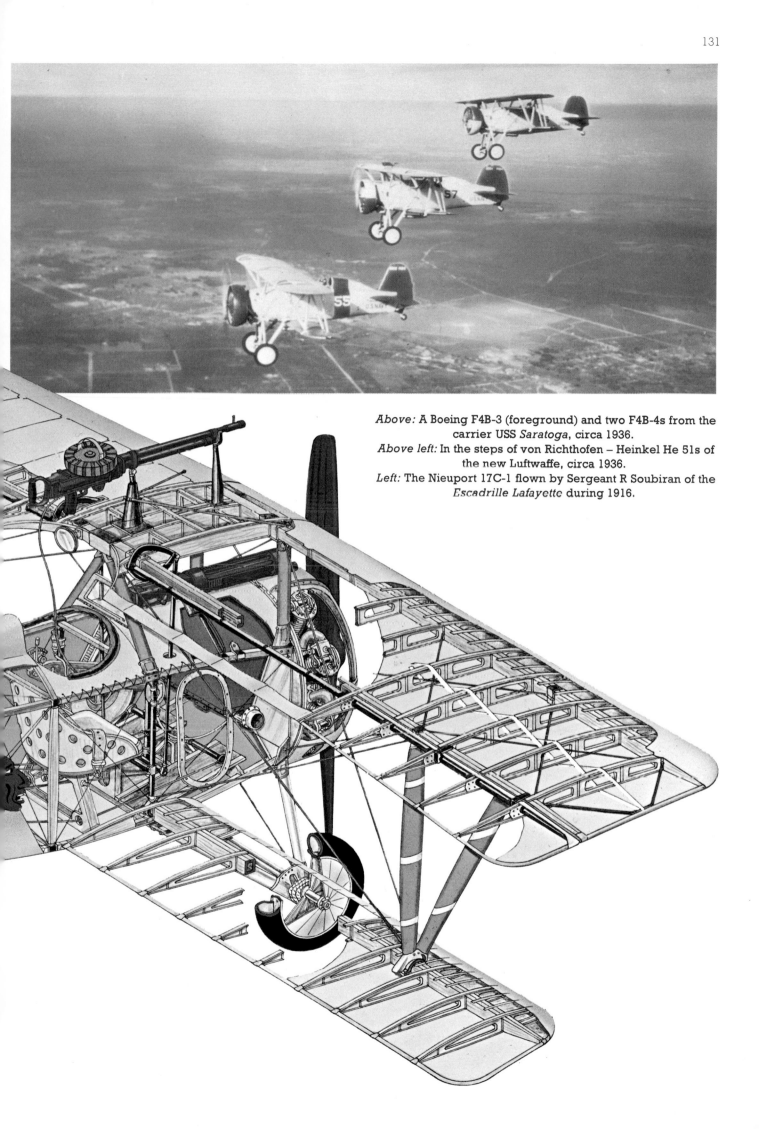

Above: A Boeing F4B-3 (foreground) and two F4B-4s from the carrier USS *Saratoga*, circa 1936.
Above left: In the steps of von Richthofen – Heinkel He 51s of the new Luftwaffe, circa 1936.
Left: The Nieuport 17C-1 flown by Sergeant R Soubiran of the *Escadrille Lafayette* during 1916.

temporary conditions, leaving only one other possible answer to such a problem – increase the number of guns fitted to any fighter.

The basic question of improved ammunition was mainly allied to the main difference between construction methods and materials used in wartime aircraft and new designs coming into service by 1930. Whereas the vast majority of 1914–18 aircraft had been fabric-skinned box structures of wood or light alloy tubing, the main trend for aircraft construction by 1930 was toward all-metal aircraft, with fabric skinning applied only to control surfaces such as ailerons and elevators. Thus the destructive power of obsolete ammunition lessened considerably against the latest aircraft types entering service. Some consideration was given to the use of heavier-caliber shell cannons in most air forces, but, for example, the RAF still retained rifle-caliber guns and ammunition in its fighters until at least 1941, with only solitary exceptions. Even thereafter most RAF fighters used throughout 1939–45 employed a mixture of the same outdated machine guns and 20 mm cannons, despite the fact that the latter weapon had been rejected by German aircraft designers as obsolete by 1939! In the United States similar dogged adherence to outmoded armament plagued

true progression of American fighters (and, indeed, bombers) until late in World War II.

A glance at the front-line fighters of the world's air forces circa 1930 reveals only too plainly the glue-footed rate of 'progress' in design and conception. The RAF's meager force of home defense fighters was equipped with Gloster Gamecocks, Bristol Bulldogs and Armstrong Whitworth Siskin IIIa – all biplanes of conventional configuration, each armed with twin .303 machine guns, and none capable of exceeding 170 mph at best with a full 'war load.' Nor was the immediate future much brighter. By September 1932 Britain's air defense fighter arm comprised a total of 13 squadrons; 10 of these were still equipped with Bulldogs, and the remaining trio with Hawker Fury I interceptors – the first RAF fighter in service able to exceed 200 mph fully loaded. Its armament, however, remained just two .303 machine guns. Each of these designs was renowned in particular for its fluid maneuverability, an asset betraying a designers' fixation with fighting tactical requirements chained to the 1918 conception of dogfighting. Though still necessary by the 1930s, such tactics were being steadily outmoded as speeds topped the 200-mph mark. Such maneuverability, however, found its niche' in the contemporary fetish in the RAF for

aerobatic displays, formation shows and other forms of aerial showmanship, both within Service circles and especially at the annual RAF Displays held at Hendon, London, for the benefit of the tax-paying public. Their American counterparts were chiefly the Curtiss Hawk and Boeing P-12 series, again, biplanes, twin-gunned, and with maximum speeds well below the 200-mph level. Here, too, much accent was given to 'parade-ground' flying – neat, pretty formation flying, embellished by colorful squadron insignia and markings, presenting an appearance of immaculate efficiency to the layman onlooker.

Delightful both to fly and watch, such biplane fighters offered performance ranges of ceiling, climb and speed only marginally better than the latest bomber designs in, or about to enter, service. An outstanding illustration of the capabilities of a well-engined, carefully designed bomber far superior to even its contemporary first-line fighters was the Fairey Fox which made its first flight on 3 January 1925, and in the following year

Right: **Wringing out a sleek Hawker Fury I.**
Below: **Grumman XSF-2, a 1931 design for a naval two-seat 'scout,' demonstrating its retractable undercarriage and lowered arrester hook for deck landing.**

Far left: Leutnant Arthur Laumann (who achieved 26 victories) of Jasta 10, 'Richthofen Circus,' in 1918 in his Fokker D VII.
Left: A neat line-up of Fokker D XVII twin-gun fighters of the Luchtvaartafdeling (Netherlands Air Force) circa 1934. Maximum speed was only barely in excess of 200 mph.
Right: The Bristol Type 123 of 1934 was intended as a four-gun day-and-night fighter. Not accepted for production, it was the last Bristol biplane to be built at Filton.

equipped just one squadron, No. 12, in the RAF. The Fox's clean nose design and 480-hp Curtiss D-12 engine gave it a top speed in excess of 150 mph, enabling it to outspace any RAF fighter of its day. As far as the RAF was concerned, this disparity between fighter and bomber performance was to steadily widen until the biplane interceptor was finally superseded by Hurricanes and Spitfires in 1938–39. The last open-cockpit biplane fighter to see RAF squadron use was the Gloster Gauntlet, which commenced its Service life with 19 Squadron at Duxford in May 1935. With a service ceiling of 33,000 feet and a top speed of 230 mph, the Gauntlet was nevertheless merely another twin-gun armed fighter, and had the same weaponry power as its lineal predecessor the SE5a of 1917. The ultimate biplane fighter of any type to enter RAF firstline service was a stablemate, the Gloster Gladiator, which was first received by 3 Squadron in March 1937. Of roughly comparable performance to the Gauntlet, albeit some 20 mph faster, the Gladiator had at least the saving grace of heavier armament – four .303 machine guns, two in the fuselage and one under each wing. Both Gloster biplanes remained in first-line service until the outbreak of war with Germany in September 1939, at which time they represented some 30 percent of RAF Fighter Command's overall stock of aircraft, though only approximately 14 percent of the command's actual operational strength on the squadrons.

The trend in American fighter design by the early 1930s was already swinging to the monoplane, one of the best-known of

Above: The Fokker Dr1, triplane of Jagdstaffel II, which was flown by Manfred von Richthofen, the Red Baron.

these being the Boeing P-26 single-wing pursuit, known affectionately to its crews as the 'Peashooter.' Deliveries of the squat little monoplane began in December 1933, and with this low-winged, all-metal monoplane fighter the US Army Air Corps finalized its transition from the past decades of biplane pre-domination. Within three years faster, better-armed monoplane pursuits were succeeding the P-26, in particular, the Curtiss P-36 Hawk and Seversky's bulky P-35, variants of both reaching squadrons prior to the United States' eventual involvement in the European war. Almost parallel to America in progressing rapidly from biplane to monoplane fighters (and bombers) was the clandestine German air service. By 1933 the secret training base at Lipezk in Russia had completed its overall task of nurturing a future Luftwaffe, and new air-training stations had been established on German soil. In existence by then were several so-termed 'Advertising Detachments,' in effect squadron nucleii at near-full strength. From them the first fighter squadron was formed, No. 132, at Döberitz, near Berlin, commencing 1 April 1934. It was commanded by Major Ritter von Greim, a World War I fighter ace, and was equipped with Arado Ar 64 and Ar 65 biplanes. Then by a decree dated 26 February 1935, the *Reichsluftwaffe* – Hitler's own title for the reborn German air service, which came to be called simply Luftwaffe – came into open recognition. On 14 March 1935 No. 132 Squadron was given the title *Jagdgeschwader Richthofen Nr 2*, comprised of two groups equipped with Arado Ar 65s and Heinkel He 51s at Döberitz and Jüterborg respectively, with the ex-1918 *Richthofen Geschwader* ace Arthur Laumann in overall command.

With the huge advantages accruing from a fresh aviation industry geared to production primarily for equipping the new German air forces, the change from biplanes to monoplanes could be accomplished relatively quickly, and by 1937 the *JG2 Richthofen* pilots were converting from their already-obsolete biplanes onto first examples of production Messerschmitt Bf 109 all-metal monoplane fighters. If the response of the young German fighter pilots to their new 'steeds' was one of eager enthusiasm, it was a feeling not wholly shared by an older generation of pilots. Men like Ernst Udet, the 62-victory ace of 1914–18 who, upon climbing out of the enclosed cockpit of the first Bf 109, remarked, 'This will never make a fighter. A pilot needs an open cockpit. He has to feel the air rushing by. And you should install a second wing above, with struts in between. . . .' Such an outmoded bias came from a man who, within two years, was to be appointed head of the Luftwaffe's technical services, with ultimate responsibility for all matters of equipment and procurement. Udet's opposition to enclosed cockpits in fighters was echoed in Britain by the (then) head of the RAF's fighter arm, Air Chief Marshal Sir Robert Brooke-Popham, when the first specifications were issued for what was to emerge as the Supermarine Spitfire. Such men had learned their 'seat-of-the-pants' flying in the wicker-cane seats of trusted and tried multiplane aircraft, aircraft which had somehow transmitted the true feel of flying to pilots and almost made them one with nature. An open cockpit had literally put them in constant touch with this element of nature which man was newly challenging. After years of such experience the claustrophobic restriction of an enclosed canopy immediately robbed such pilots of that personal contact and therefore destroyed an intimacy impossible to achieve at such a level in any plexiglass panoply.

With rare exceptions the biplane fighter had been 'retired' by 1939 in all nations' air services – at least, ostensibly – though in actual practice many hundreds of obsolete examples were to soldier on in varying degrees almost throughout World War II. Such designs were patently outdated in the quicksilver pace of air fighting inherent with modern warfare. The era of man-versus-man dogfighting, epitomized in the high air over France in 1917 and 1918, was now history, merely one more chapter in human progress.

Above: The last of the RAF's open-cockpit biplane fighters, the Gloster Gauntlet equipped many RAF squadrons from 1935, and a few examples were still on active strength abroad as late as 1943. This formation bears the blue and white checker markings of 19 Squadron, RAF.

Below: Gloster Sea Gladiator, N5525, shows its 'underskirts,' including the two underwing gun housings and vee-type arrester hook at the rear fuselage.

Big Brothers

Fascination with huge airplane designs is traceable almost to the start of man-controlled flight. Grasping the basic outline of the larger soaring birds, man attempted to copy such surface areas in the firm belief that greater area meant more successful flight. In terms of the powered airplane the world's truly big aircraft all stem from one design, the Russian Sikorsky-designed *Le Grand* of 1913. In August of that year, only three months after its first flight, it set a world endurance record of nearly two airborne hours, carrying eight people and reaching an altitude of 2723 feet (830 m). Powered by four 100-hp engines, *Le Grand* also incorporated a totally enclosed cabin and dual controls, and its rectangular wings spanned almost 93 feet. From it was built an even more luxurious giant, the *Ilya Muromets*, which first flew in January 1914, the precursor of some 80 further examples which entered service with the military as bombers when the *Eskadra Vozdushnykh Korablei* (Squadron of Flying Ships) was formed at the start of 1915. This unit – the world's first *heavy* bomber unit – commenced operations in February 1915, and before the 1917 revolution in Russia had flown some 400 bombing sorties over German and Lithuanian territories. Apart from many innovations for crew comfort, the *Ilya Muromets* could dispense a bomb load of some 1500 pounds (almost 700 kg), using Russian-designed bomb sights, and carried between three and seven defensive machine gunners, including a tail gunpit.

The possibilities of aerial bombing had not been lost in other countries at that time. At the start of the war France formed several Voisin-equipped *escadrilles* tasked with bombing which became the nucleus of a 1915 force of 600 such bombers.

In Britain both its air services, the RFC and RNAS, adapted existing two-seat reconnaissance airplanes to carry small loads of 20-pound Hales bombs, usually hand-dropped or cable-released from crude 'carrier' attachments under wings or fuselage. The main initiative for an offensive bombing policy against German targets must be credited to the Air Department of the Admiralty, commanded then by Commodore Murray Seuter, RN. Commencing in September 1914, small formations – often only three or four aircraft – proceeding individually from the RNAS units in Belgium attempted bombing attacks on known Zeppelin airship bases, raids attended by some success. The commander of the RNAS detachment in Belgium, the fiery Charles Rumsey Samson, sent a request to the Admiralty for a 'bloody paralyser' of an airplane, hopefully to retard the German advance on Antwerp. This colorful 'requirement' was passed via Seuter to the Handley Page Company, who undertook to build a huge (wing-span of 114 feet) Type O biplane bomber, with twin engines, capable of lifting 600 pounds of bombs. The first prototype 'O,' No. 1455, was completed in November 1915, made its first flights the next month, and other examples began to be delivered to RNAS units from May 1916, albeit sporadically. In service the giant Handley Page was titled HP O/100, and its wing span was 100 feet. The first O/100 bombing sortie took place on the night of 16 March 1917 when O/100, No. 1460 of 3 Wing RNAS dropped 12 × 100-pound bombs on Moulin-les-Metz rail station.

In Germany, too, thoughts for truly large, long-range aircraft were being crystallized into fact with the earliest Gotha designs, rumbling behemoths which presaged the later Gotha and

Above: Staaken R.VI (Schül) 29/16 R-plane which saw operational use with Rfa.501 and eventually crash-landed in fog at Scheldewindeke on 10 May 1918. Its wings spanned some 140 feet and takeoff weight was about 11,500 kg.
Right: Caproni Ca 5 of the Corpo Aeronautica Militare (Italian Air Corps) of 1918. A three-engined – the third unit is behind the pilots cockpit, thus hidden in this view – bomber used for long, arduous raids over mountainous regions in the Italian – Austro-Hungarian conflict.

Riesenflugzeug (Giant Airplane) raiders over England in 1917–18. This latter R-Class of great-sized biplane bombers was initiated in the opening months of the war, when construction commenced on the first of a line of Staaken R-Class aircraft. In the meantime Siemens-Schuckert engaged the Steffen brothers to pursue the pair's ideas in a prewar design for a similarly big aircraft. In the marine aviation field, almost simultaneously, Count Zeppelin commissioned Claude Dornier to produce his eventual all-metal R-Class seaplanes. Despite the huge variety of technical difficulties facing such designers – there were virtually no precedents – progress was astonishingly quick,

Right: The giant Sikorsky-designed *Russki Vityaz* (Russian Knight) bomber of 1913, with ski undercarriage. Powered by four 100-hp Argus engines mounted along lower wings, it carried a crew of seven, plus a 'useful' (sic) load of 1540 pounds. It was wrecked in a midair collision in the 1913 Russian military trials.
Below: The ill-fated Kennedy Giant.

and the first German 'Giant' was available for operations by late 1915, followed by the first successful operational sortie recorded in August 1916. In the interim, however, isolated bombing raids had been accomplished against English targets by more 'normal' two-seat biplanes on isolated occasions from late 1914. Then, on 28 November 1916, Leutnant Walter Ilges and Deck Officer Paul Brandt took off from Mariakerke in an LVG two-seater, reached southwest London by noon, and scattered six 20-pound bombs around the Victoria Station area – London's first airplane bombing attack. Some months later *The Times* newspaper was to comment, describing this audacious sortie as an event '. . . of most significance (*that year*) to the future of humanity' – prophetic words which, largely, went unheeded.

If the British civil population tended at the time to dismiss such raids as mere stunts, and continued to regard the German rigid airships – Zeppelins – as the prime menace, such euphoria was swiftly dispelled on 25 May 1917. On that day a loose gaggle of 21 Gothas coolly paraded over Folkestone and released over 5000 kg of bombs, killing 95 people and further injuring 195 in the space of a few minutes. The assault literally came out of the blue – unheralded and totally unexpected. A further raid on Sheerness followed on 5 June, but on 13 June 17 Gothas calmly flew in broad daylight over the British capital, London, dropped 4400 kg of bombs, and caused casualties of 162 killed and 432 others injured. Forty-six of the overall total were children below the age of five who were together in an infants' school struck by a single bomb. No previous air raid, whether by airship or airplane had caused such a total human toll. The Gothas were all from *Kampfgeschwader 3* – the so-termed 'England Squadron,' formed specifically to undertake long-range strategical bombing forays against England. These intrepid crews were to continue their raids against English civil targets for one year, reverting to night sorties in the later stages. Their depredations – albeit relatively small in sheer statistical contexts – were largely responsible for, among other matters, the amalgamation of Britain's RFC and RNAS, into a third, independent service, the Royal Air Force which came into being from 1 April 1918.

The problems of operating such unprecedented large aircraft over long-range flights, which included much of such a flight over the cold waters of the lower North Sea, were myriad. The aircraft themselves required constant control, involving – in most cases – exhausting physical effort on pilots' part. The added problems of fatigue, lack of heating and oxygen increased the predictable stress and fatigue for all crew members. Parachutes were never carried – there seemed little point in these on prolonged over-water sorties – while radio sets were of prohibitive weight and therefore omitted from the essential equipment of the bombers. The normal hazards of any long sortie over enemy territory were compounded by the ever-uncertain weather conditions. Nevertheless, the crews of these Gothas and R-Class mammoths created a form of aerial warfare with which the Allied air forces finally crippled the German nation less than 30 years later.

The Allied air services were, in the main, slow to exploit the possibilities of the true heavy bomber. An inkling of the potential of strategic bombing was exemplified in the 1916 formation of No. 3 Wing RNAS, a combined Anglo-French force of 'normal' two-seat bombers tasked with assaulting German industrial objectives within a limited range. The only large aircraft used were the first examples of the Handley Page O/100 (as previously detailed) and a particularly cumbersome biplane, the Short Bomber. The latter was, initially, a straight conversion of the Short 184 float-plane into a land-based machine, and first examples were produced early in 1916. The type entered service with 7 Wing, RNAS at Coudekerque in November 1916, and some 15 machines were allotted to 3 Wing, RNAS, while a handful were pressed into RFC use ostensibly to assist in the Somme battles that autumn. Its upper wing spanned 84 feet (25.6 m), and its usual bomb load comprised eight 65-pound bombs, but its elephantine handling characteristics and generally low performance range condemned the type for widespread employment. The mainstay of 3 Wing, RNAS's bombers were adapted Sopwith two-seaters, combined with such ungainly French 'pushers' as the Breguet-Michelins – aircraft with severely limited bomb-carrying capacity and operational range, and possessing performance ranges which left them at the mercy of any attacking German fighters. Defensive armament was basically a hand-operated machine gun. By June 1917 No. 3 Wing had been disbanded, but a successor, the 41st Wing, RFC was formed in its place and commenced operations in the same role in October 1917, flying De Havilland 4s and FE2bs. Retitled VIII Brigade, RAF in May 1918, it was in turn replaced in June 1918 by the formation of the Independent Force, RAF, commanded by Hugh Trenchard.

Above: Possibly the best of the US Army Air Corps' biplane bombers was the B-2 Condor which came into service in the early 1930s.
Left: The US Army's first aerial giant bomber, the Whiteman XNBL-1, or as it was more popularly nicknamed 'Barling Bomber' (after its designer Walter Barling) and 'Mitchell's Folly' (after its chief sponsor General 'Billy' Mitchell). It first flew in 1923, but its pathetic performance led to its abandonment by 1925.
Below: The three-seat, twin-engined Letord 2 bomber project for the French air services of 1916–17. Its successor, the Letord 3, was the first true bomber of this development line.

Equipped in the main with De Havilland 4 and DH9 two-seat bombers, the Independent Force also used the heavy HP O/100 and O/400 variants, bombers (in the latter case) which on occasion lifted the huge 1650-pound SN bomb for raids on German communications and industry. Still pressing for greater range and effect for strategic operations, a new formation, No. 27 Group, RAF was inaugurated, consisting (on paper, at least) of three fresh squadrons, intended for equipment with the HP V/1500 bomber. A logical development of the HP O/400, the V/1500, was powered by four engines (in tandem pairs) offering at least 1500 hp (hence the aircraft's designation), had an equal wing-span of 126 feet (38.4 m), and was originally intended to carry a bomb load up to 28×112 pounds. Envisaged as capable of bombing Berlin from bases in East Anglia, the V/1500 was also mooted as a carrier for the 3300-pound bomb then being designed. The opportunity to put all these highly theoretical operational 'assets' into practice never presented itself, however, due to the signing of an armistice with the Central Powers on 11 November 1918. Another design, from which much was expected, was the Vickers FB27 Vimy, a twin-engined bomber of which more than 1000 were contracted for construction in early 1918. During initial testing, the prototype Vimy demon-

strated an ability to lift twice the load of an HP O/400, could achieve a speed of 100 mph, and had a calculated endurance of about 11 hours fully loaded. Only one Vimy ever reached the fighting zone in France, just prior to the Armistice, and this highly promising design never saw action during the war. The Vimy's true niche in aviation annals was to come in the post-1918 era as the vehicle in which several record long-distance flights were accomplished, including the first direct aerial crossing of the north Atlantic in 1919 by John Alcock and Arthur Whitten Brown.

Though Russia and Germany, and tardily Britain, had blazed the pathway forward for large bombers and their strategic usage, Italy also played an important part in such progress. In

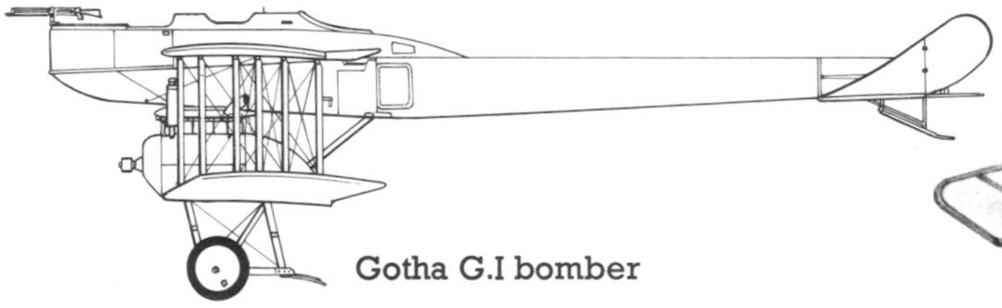

Gotha G.I bomber

Gotha G.II bomber

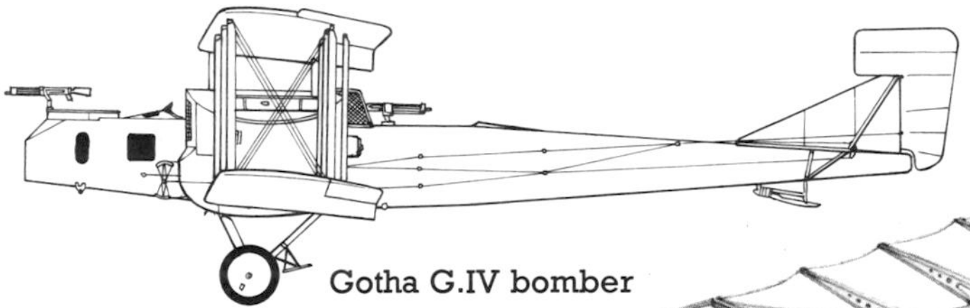

Gotha G.IV bomber

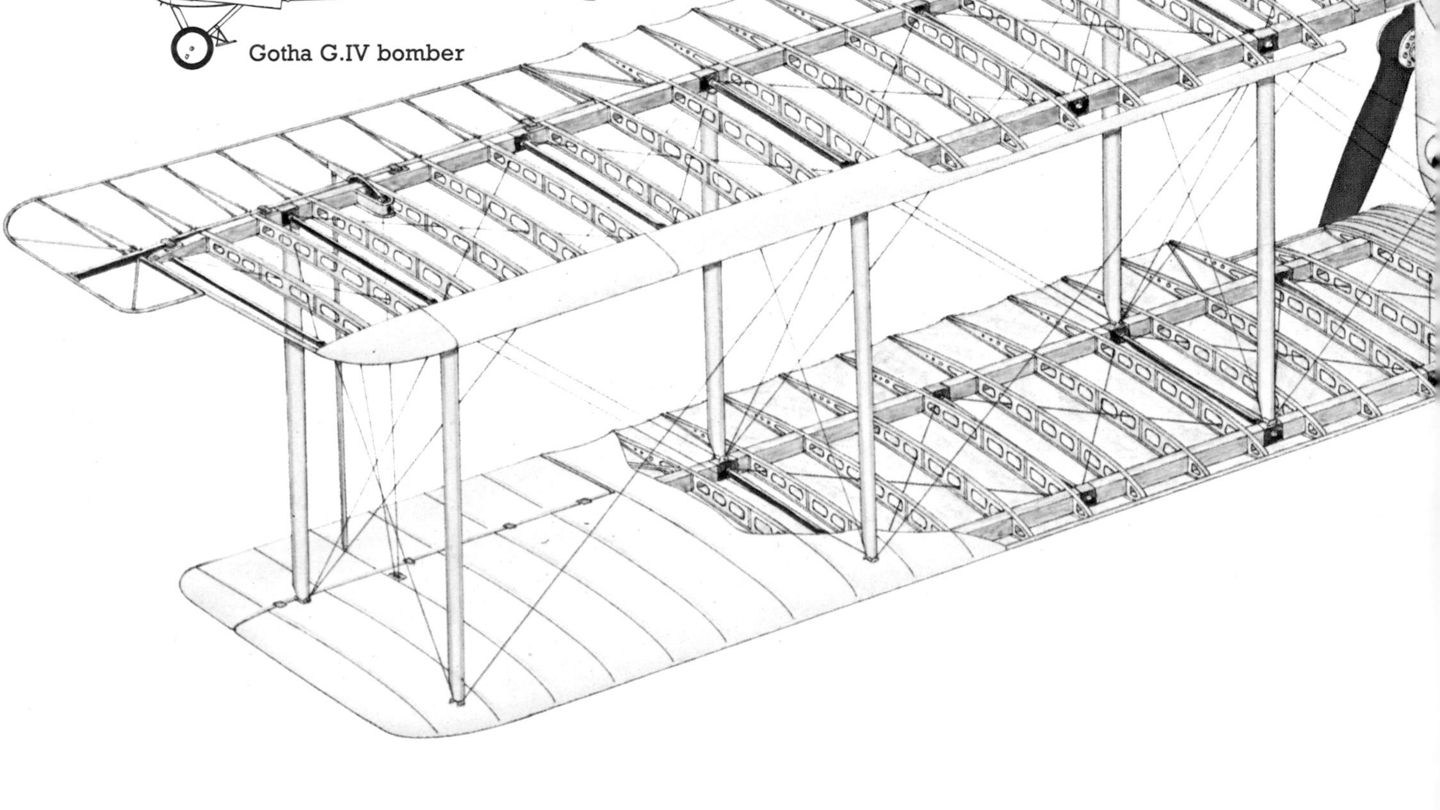

particular the various Caproni biplane and triplane bombers were used to good effect in long-range, strategic sorties, the first such missions being flown as early as 20 August 1915. Their successes were especially praiseworthy in view of the difficult, mountainous regions over which they were forced to fly in their offensive against Austro-Hungarian targets. Such successful bomber designs represented merely the tip of a host of other, less worthy aircraft built experimentally, even hopefully, by all nations throughout the war. The international quest for ideal war machines gave loose license to many individual aircraft manufacturers and designers – often merely enthusiasts with sufficient finance and contacts to interest governmental departments in their highly individual efforts – to construct airplanes which, patently, had little hope of practical use in the white-hot crucible of active operations. One example of such 'blind alley' projects was the British Kennedy Giant. Designed by an Englishman, C J H Mackenzie-Kennedy, who had assisted Igor Sikorsky in Russia pre-1914 in producing the *Ilya Muromets*, he began assembly of the many component sections – made by other established firms – at Northolt in late 1916. Delays and difficulties retarded completion of the Giant until late 1917 when, due mainly to grossly underpowered engines, the mammoth simply baffled all attempts to get it airborne. With its 142-foot

Top: The Fairey Fox two-seat day bomber which created a sensation when first demonstrated to RAF hierarchy.
Left: The Gotha G.IV of Bombengeschwader 3 based at Ghent, used for daylight raids over southern England during the summer of 1917.
Below: A Vickers Vernon, named *Pelican*, of 45 Squadron, RAF, with King Feisal of Jordan in the cockpit.

Gotha G.Vb bomber

span wings and lengthy box-like fuselage, distinctly reminiscent of its Sikorsky antecedent, the earthbound Giant remained rotting at Northolt for several years – a mute monument to failure.

With the cessation of hostilities in November 1918, war-weary governments allowed almost all proceeding manufacture of bombers (and other military aircraft) to decline, and most nations turned their attention to the prospects of commercial aviation, rather than military progress. The immediate means for undertaking civil air routes was provided in all cases by existing heavy bombers which, with relatively small effort and expense, could be converted to passenger carriage and/or freight haulage. This was particularly true of the bigger bombers which had only recently emerged from their manufacturers – aircraft ready-tested and proven and which, denuded of warlike hardware became instant airliners. One such was the rectangular Farman F.60 *Goliath* designed in 1918 as a bomber, which was quickly 'civilianized' and then gave splendid service in every corner of the globe until at least 1933. In Britain many of the wartime-designed Handley Page O/400 bombers were similarly pressed into civilian garb.

Of the many new designs of 1918, too late to see war service, a relative few entered service use during the immediate post-1918 years. One example was the Vickers Vimy which first equipped 58 Squadron RAF in Egypt in mid-1919; another was the De Havilland 10 which gave brief service at squadron level both at home and overseas. By 1925, however, many RAF heavy night-bomber squadrons were receiving factory-fresh examples of a new bomber, the Vickers Virginia, a trundling twin-engined biplane which eventually gave some 13 years' doughty service in its many variants. In the same year the dogged persistence of Hugh Trenchard, exponent of an independent air service and a prophet of the unlimited destructive potential of air power, finally obtained agreement of the Air Ministry for an expansion of the RAF to an eventual strength of 52 first-line squadrons – two-thirds of the force to be equipped with bombers. The emphasis on bomber strength merely exemplified Trenchard's unwavering policy of offense being the finest form of defense. The year 1925 also witnessed a shattering of complacency among Air Ministry hierarchy about bomber design in general, for in January 1925 the original Fairey Fox two-seat day bomber made its initial flights. Financed and developed privately by the Fairey Company, the Fox employed an American Curtiss D-12 in-line engine, Curtiss-Reed metal propeller, and its general outline had been 'cleaned up' to a high degree with an eye to maximum speed and efficiency. Demonstrated to Trenchard in October 1925, the Fox was immediately contracted for production to equip a complete squadron, No. 12. Its aerodynamically efficient design and engine installation gave the Fox a speed margin of some 40 mph minimum over existing RAF bombers – *and* fighters!

The impact of the Fox on British officialdom was to provide a belated stimulus to continued development of modern bomber

Above left: Makeshift 'bomber' – a Curtiss-Wright T-32 Condor in Chinese national markings with (apparently) bombs under its wings.
Above: Handley Page Hyderabads of 99 Squadron, RAF in stepped-down echelon formation.
Right: The Ninak's stoic companion on RAF operations around the world from 1917–32 was the Bristol F2b, which became a jack-of-all-trades in many, varied roles. This example, F4463, belonged to 31 Squadron in India.

designs – apart from its overt epitomization of the results possible from private enterprise in a field which, normally, *should* have been the whole concern of an air service's administrative body. The contemporary sloth in governmental circles at that time was primarily a product of the contemporary European euphoria of disarmament policies being sought. In 1926, however, the RAF began receiving a new medium (sic) bomber, the Boulton and Paul Sidestrand – the service's first twin-engined biplane bomber since the 1918 DH 10. In the same year an Air Ministry Specification No. 12/26 was issued to certain manufacturers for a two-seat, high performance day-bomber design. Of the various projects derived one was the superlative Hawker Hart, destined to be the progenitor of a long line of classic biplane bombers used by the RAF almost up to World War II. The first Hart prototype made its maiden flight in June 1928, and 33 Squadron was the first squadron to be re-equipped with Harts, in January 1930. Capable of a speed in excess of 180 mph with full warload, highly maneuverable, and of sleek outline, the Hart set a new pattern for RAF bombers.

In the heavy bomber class the RAF continued to employ the drag-inducing, cumbersome biplane configuration until well into the 1930s. While single squadrons continued to receive such contemporary designs as Handley Page Hyderabads and Hinaidis, Boulton and Paul Overstrands, and other one-off types, the veteran Vickers Virginia remained first-line squadron equipment in several units until as late as 1934 before finally being replaced – and only then by another 'canvas bomber.' The 'Ginnie's' main successor was the Handley Page Heyford, which entered service in November 1933. The Heyford – the RAF's ultimate biplane heavy bomber – soldiered on until 1939 before finally quitting front-line service in favor of recently introduced all-metal, monoplane 'heavies.' Though somewhat unorthodox in design, the Heyford's top speed of 140 mph at best, hand-operated, open cockpit defensive gun positions, and modest range of approximately 900 miles with a 1500-pound bomb load, were reminiscent of 1918 concept bombers. Such had been the tardy progression of the RAF's envisaged

Right: The vintage De Havilland 9A – Ninak to its crews – soldiered on in RAF operational units until the early 1930s. This tight line-abreast comprised DH9As of 47 Squadron from Helwan, Egypt circa 1926. Note the spare wheels slung *under* fuselages.

K
4546

46

'offensive bomber' progression during the locust years of peace.

In America the armistice of 1918 brought an abrupt end to several years of painfully slow buildup of aerial strength and aviation industry. And with the coming of peace the main tenor of American higher policy was a return to the isolationism from 'outer world' politics from which it had been dragged reluctantly in 1916–17. In the context of military air strength and potential progress, therefore, there seemed little basis for any great effort – or expense – in equipping its air arm with up-to-date aircraft. A huge war-surplus stock of American, British and German designs from the war appeared adequate to use in an air service rapidly demobilized to a personnel strength of merely 10,000 by 1920, supporting some two dozen first-line squadrons attached to various Army corps. America's isolation, both politically and geographically, especially affected the future of the American bomber. Pundits in military circles, encrusted with traditional army and naval thinking, regarded the United States' physical estrangement from Europe and Asia as sufficient proof of its natural defense against any aerial assault – quite logically in view of the airplane's infancy at that stage. They therefore expressed no interest in building any strong, or independent, air arm. One outstanding exception to such rutted thinking was Colonel W E 'Billy' Mitchell, an American Army officer who had served in France and witnessed the power of aircraft. Appointed Director of Military Aeronautics in 1919, Mitchell, an open admirer of the RAF's Hugh Trenchard and the latter's advocacy of offensive air-power potential, began a lifelong crusade for an independent US air service, well-equipped with bombers. His vision, if sometimes misguided in execution and details, was broadly vindicated in 1941 when Japanese aircraft all but nullified US military and naval dominance in the Pacific. His first attempts to stir action for re-equipping the meager air corps resulted in the production of a giant triplane bomber, the Whiteman XNBL-1, more popularly titled the Barling Bomber after its designer Walter Barling, which eventually appeared in mid-1923. Results of the Barling's test flights condemned the mammoth aircraft as inferior in all respects to the existing Martin MB-2 bomber, particularly in respect of range and speed. The project was promptly abandoned, and became known as 'Mitchell's Folly' thereafter.

Still relentlessly pursuing his campaign for better air power for America, Mitchell's next major step was to arrange a practical demonstration of his contention that large naval vessels, that is, battleships, were outmoded for war by the advent of the bomber. Using several surrendered German

Left: The angular Boulton Paul Overstrand equipped only one squadron, No. 101 (illustrated), but pioneered the power-driven gun turret for heavy bombers.
Below: The Hart J9941, painted in 57 Squadron's pre-1939 colors, preserved at the RAF Museum, Hendon.

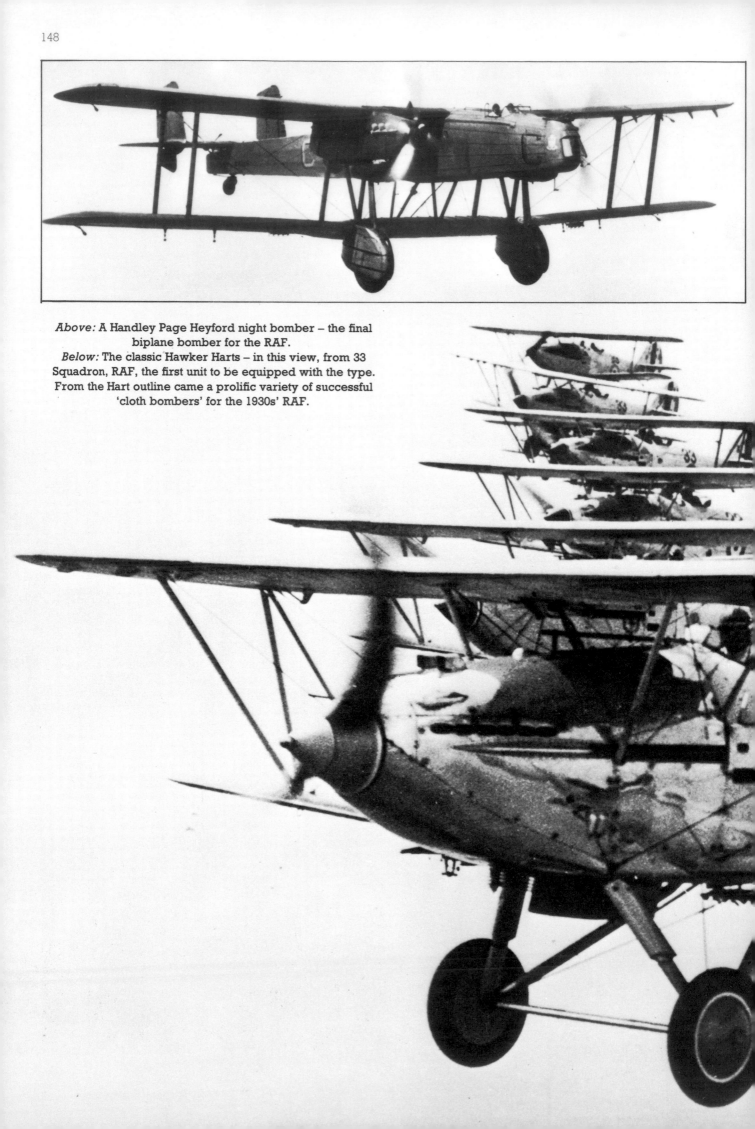

Above: A Handley Page Heyford night bomber – the final biplane bomber for the RAF.

Below: The classic Hawker Harts – in this view, from 33 Squadron, RAF, the first unit to be equipped with the type. From the Hart outline came a prolific variety of successful 'cloth bombers' for the 1930s' RAF.

battleships as the bait, moored off Virgina Capes, a force of naval and army aircraft proceeded to bomb and sink three of the vessels with direct hits during July 1921, and a fourth in resumed trials in the following September. The main successes were obtained by the army Martin MB-2s; the last sinking being achieved with a 2000-pound bomb specially made for the occasion. If Mitchell had demonstrably illustrated his constant theme, little notice was taken by the naval powers, though with hindsight it is now possible to trace a subtle, fresh outlook on naval strategy from this point on. Mitchell's parallel quest for an autonomous air force also foundered on the reefs of hardened traditional Army opposition; the only concession was a retitling of the land-based air service as the Army Air Corps from 1926.

At that date the airmen were still relying to a great extent on wartime designs, with a supplementing force of the aging Martin bomber. Replacements for the latter came in 1927 with the Keystone LB-5, a steel-framed, fabric-skinned biplane of little advance in performance. In 1928 came another fresh design, the Curtiss B-2 Condor, with twin liquid-cooled engines, faster than any Keystone and offering twice the range. Limited funds led to the Air Corps preferring the much cheaper Keystone, however, and only relatively few Condors entered service with the bombardment squadrons. The substantial advantages in speed and maneuverability of contemporary

pursuit (fighter) designs added credence to the thought that fighter offense could always destroy or at least disperse any bomber formation. This theory was overtly true of the aircraft in service in 1930, but by 1933 American aviation was swinging determinedly toward the monoplane in all aspects. The Army Air Corps squadrons then began receiving Martin B-12s from 1934 – all-metal, twin-engined, monowing bombers capable of speeds beyond 200 mph, and incorporating cupola-protected defensive gun positions. Then in June 1934 the Boeing Company was contracted to produce a four-engined, monoplane bomber able to lift 8000 pounds of bombs over very long ranges. The eventual result was the Boeing XB-15, 'father' of the legendary B-17 Flying Fortress of World War II fame. Such developments, in parallel with a similar advance in fighter designs, echoed the demise of the biplane bomber in the American services.

The worldwide general reluctance by governmental departments to sponsor, or at least encourage, progressive development of the post-1918 airplane was strongly reflected in the longevity in active life of such ostensibly 'new' aircraft as the biplane bombers which commenced military careers throughout the 1920s and – in too many cases – the 1930s. With rare exception such 'canvas' bombers were merely minimally improved over the designs which had pioneered strategic bombing in 1917–18. The admirable service these gave in those

peace years was, in part, a tribute to the patience and skills of contemporary designers who were cramped by officialdom's parsimony and lack of either enthusiasm and/or technical expertise in aeronautical fields. It was even more an accolade for the young bomber crews who were compelled to attempt to implement the latest theories on bombing strategy and tactics in aircraft well outdated for the task. Yet from the ranks of those bomber boys were to come the senior officers who, in the years 1939–45, conducted the strategic bombing offensive against Nazi Germany which contributed heavily to the utter defeat of Hitler's vaunted '1000-year Reich.'

Warriors All

The commonest conception of biplanes at war is almost wholly associated with the aerial conflict of 1914–18. Yet in the broader history of multiwing aircraft those years saw merely the first 'blooding' of the biplane. From 1918 until the late 1940s biplanes figured prominently in dozens of minor wars and other warlike operations in virtually every corner of the globe. The 1918 armistice between the major warring nations was a signal for a number of internal European struggles, mainly countries attempting to achieve independence from former rulers. In Poland, Latvia and Estonia, for example, aerial fighting continued for nearly three years between various factions, and former wartime aircraft flew again in combat. In South Russia the struggle between ex-Czarist sympathizers and the Bolshevik revolutionaries involved both sides in a continuing air war, including several RAF units dispatched by Britain in the vain hope of propping up the defunct White Russian cause. Nevertheless, the prime example of an almost nonstop operational effort in the so-termed 'peace' years between the two

greatest wars of this century was Britain's RAF. Charged with responsibility for governing or controlling vast areas of Empire or mandated territories, Britain quickly turned to its air services as the sharp end of military control. The chief zones for such consideration were several countries bordering the Mediterranean and Red Sea, and the troubled regions of India's Northwest Frontier Province (now called Pakistan).

For the first decade of the post-1918 era the bulk of such RAF operations were undertaken by two wartime-designed types, the De Havilland 9A – or 'Ninak' in RAF parlance – and the Bristol F2b. Both two-seaters came to be used in a variety of roles and were veritable maids-of-all-work. Flying daily over bald deserts or menacing rock mountains, their opponents were the recalcitrant local tribesmen who seldom ceased fermenting rebellions en masse against the white 'Raj' (Rule). And lest it be thought that the RAF crews had a sinecure in view of a total lack of aerial opposition, it might be of interest to note that in the widespread Arab revolt of 1919–20, during some 4000 hours flown operationally in support of the army, the handful of RAF squadrons suffered 11 aircraft shot down and a further 57 damaged and rendered unfit for flying. This was due solely to unerringly accurate groundfire by Arab riflemen. The general conditions under which the RAF operated its aging Ninaks and 'Brisfits' overseas could only properly be termed minimal – even primitive. Temperatures ranging from boiling point at airfield level to the bone-numbing cold at altitude affected both crews and aircraft – the latter's wood and fabric structures being particularly vulnerable to such extremes. Additional hazards to engines and airframes included ubiquitous sand, dust infiltration and the unforgiving barren rock landing strips in use. Attempting to achieve any worthwhile performance in the ultra-thin air was a constant nightmare to all pilots.

Such daily operations over largely uncharted desert wastelands and forbidding mountainous regions gave crews little hope of survival in the event of mechanical failure, and the parachute did not become a standard issue item to RAF crews until the late 1920s. Maintenance under such circumstances was

Right: The Supermarine Stranraer, in Canadian unit markings, now on display in the RAF Museum, Hendon.
Below: The Heinkel He 45, still in service at Prague circa 1941.

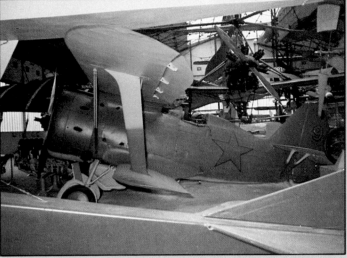

an unending labor by the indefatigable ground crews, and their task was exacerbated by a continuing lack of spares and essential equipment resulting from parsimonious budgeting for the contemporary RAF. This lack of adequate financial backing meant that the doughty DH9As and F2bs were not replaced in overseas squadrons until the late 1920s – the last first-line Bristol F2b unit was only reequipped in early 1932 – and their major replacements were Westland Wapitis and Fairey III biplanes. These too were to continue in front-line employment on operations for almost a decade. The Wapitis in India formed the original nucleus units of the Indian Air Force, and were flown operationally as late as 1940. In support of the Wapitis and, later, Hawker Harts were a number of utilitarian aircraft types which provided a form of embryo Transport Command for the Middle and Far East RAF. Foremost of these support aircraft were the various Vickers biplane transports – the Vimy, Vernon and Valentia – with added help from individual Handley Page equivalents. The Vernons and Valentias, designed and

Above left: **Russian I-152, some of which fought in Spain and particularly against the Japanese during the 1938 conflict.**
Above: **Polikarpov I-153 preserved in the French Musée de l'Air.**

used primarily for troop transportation, were also pressed into service as general freight carriers, air ambulances, and on no few occasions as heavy bombers. Their trojan, patient plodding through eastern skies proved invaluable on myriad occasions and, indeed, Valentias of 31 Squadron in India were still in operational service as late as 1942.

Apart from a measure of operational flying by Italian air force biplanes when the Italian dictator initiated his country's invasion of Abyssinia in the 1930s, the next major conflict involving combat biplanes came with the eruption of civil war in Spain. From 1936 to early 1939 the opposing air forces employed a wide variety of American, Russian, Italian and German biplanes – mainly fighters – and the ensuing, continuing combat proved

Far left: A Heinkel He 51 serving with Germany's Condor Legion in the Spanish Civil War.
Center left: The long-lived DH Tiger Moth, a type of aircraft which trained virtually the bulk of Allied pilots during World War II.
Left: A Gotha Go 145 which was delivering mail to German troops in the Channel Isles on 28 August 1940, but lost its way and landed in Sussex, England.
Below left: Supermarine Walrus amphibians of the Fleet Air Arm, a design which was used a great deal by the Air-Sea Rescue organization of the RAF and British Navy almost throughout World War II.

to be a testing ground for each contributing nation for its latest fighter (and bomber) equipment and their tactical use. In the early stages of the conflict American Boeing P-12s, Italian Fiat Cr32s, Russian I-15s, British Hawker Furies, German Heinkel He 51s, Arado Ar 68Es, and oddities such as the Fairey Feroce and even the Canadian-built Grumman FF-1 Dolphin were all pressed hastily into operational use. As the war extended, newer, faster fighters and bombers such as the Messerschmitt Bf 109 and Russian I-16 monoplanes replaced the biplanes. Germany's *Condor Legion* detachment introduced the Henschel 123 single-seat biplane to test its dive-bombing abilities, the precursor of the various *Stuka* aircraft used later in World War II. Combat generally followed tried and trusted methods first inaugurated in World War I, though at rather higher speeds. Nevertheless, the introduction of modern all-metal monoplanes quickly pointed to the obsolescence of the biplane for modern warfare. Though able to outmaneuver any high-speed monoplane, the biplane was outgunned and outflown against the sleek Messerschmitt Bf 109 or its contemporaries.

The aerial war over Spain has often been quoted, and is quoted even today, as a 'watershed' in air combat, tactically and strategically. In fact, it was basically conducted on well-tried tactical lines using methods inaugurated during 1917–18 and improved only in the light of the higher speeds and performances available from a *proportion* of the myriad aircraft types actually flown over Spain. It was, it is true, the last great aerial conflict to see purely biplane-versus-biplane combat on a grand scale, employing dogfighting tactics reminiscent of 1918. It was also a perfect 'testing ground' for 'blooding' several nations' latest monoplane fighters and bombers under ultimate operational conditions, notably the various Luftwaffe aircraft fed in to the battle spasmodically throughout 1937–38, and especially the early examples of the Bf 109 and Heinkel and Dornier bombers. The Spanish war saw the first operational use of air-to-air communications, thereby enabling the German fighter pilots to adopt fresh fighting tactical formations, including the later standard *Rotte* of pairs of fighters with one protecting the tail of the other. Despite such modern designs, however, the predominant fighter of the Spanish air war was the Italian Fiat CR32, a biplane which outnumbered its nearest 'rivals' (the Bf 109 and Heinkel He 51) by a factor of roughly four to one. Certainly, the highest-scoring fighter ace of the whole war was Garcia Morato, a Nationalist pilot, who claimed 40 combat victories by the end of the war – all in a Fiat CR32 biplane.

Though patently outdated by 1939, the biplane still figured relatively high in pure quantity in many nations' air forces as Europe exploded into its second international war of the twentieth century in September 1939. Of the major countries embroiled in the opening months of the cataclysm, for example, the Royal Air Force's Fighter Command stock of 1099 fighters included 318 Gloster Gauntlets and Gladiators. A third of these were ostensibly first-line operational types in the squadrons. Germany's Luftwaffe, still expanding to its intended ultimate strength, was in the main monoplane-equipped, yet still counted several *staffeln* of single-seat biplanes in its front-line establish-

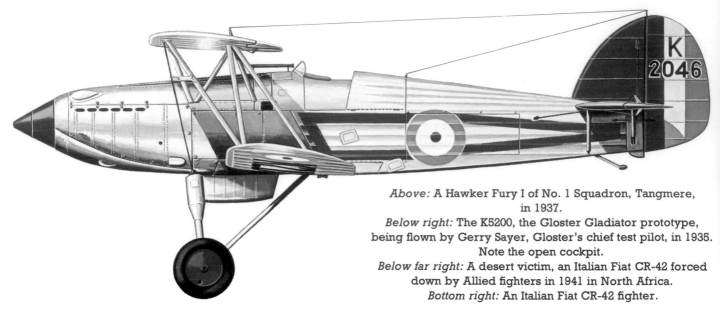

Above: A Hawker Fury I of No. 1 Squadron, Tangmere, in 1937.
Below right: The K5200, the Gloster Gladiator prototype, being flown by Gerry Sayer, Gloster's chief test pilot, in 1935. Note the open cockpit.
Below far right: A desert victim, an Italian Fiat CR-42 forced down by Allied fighters in 1941 in North Africa.
Bottom right: An Italian Fiat CR-42 fighter.

ment. Italy's *Regia Aeronautica* held 177 Fiat CR 32s in service in September 1939 and continued flying the type until early 1941, along with its stablemate the Fiat CR 42. If such fighters of yesteryear were patently overdue for replacement by updated designs, few nations could afford to withdraw them from the squadrons immediately. The crescendo of aircraft wartime production had yet to gain impetus and such stopgap aircraft were perforce vital to maintain quantitative strength.

The RAF's Gloster Gladiators comprised several squadrons in 1939–40, both in Egypt and in Britain, and these were to take a full share of the opening phases of the war in each zone. In Egypt, Palestine and the Transjordan areas of the Middle East the whole RAF fighter defenses evolved around mainly four squadrons, Nos. 33, 80, 94 and 112, each Gladiator-equipped in 1939–40. These were to fight heroic battles with both German and Italian air services as the tide of overwhelming odds gradually forced the Allied armies out of Greece, Crete and a dozen other footholds in the eastern Mediterranean. Along the North Africa coastline areas of war Gladiators also played a vital part in the aerial combats. In Europe the German invasions of Norway and other Low Countries in April 1940 saw a handful of Norwegian Gladiator pilots undertake combat against hopeless odds, while Finland's brief but intensive resistance to Russian aggression brought yet more Gladiators into first-line combat. The invasion of Norway caused Britain to dispatch No. 263 Squadron's 18 Gladiators, via aircraft carrier, in April 1940. Their initial sojourn in Norway was brief, and the personnel were soon withdrawn to Britain after claiming 14 victories. No. 263 Squadron returned to Norway with fresh Gladiators in May, and in the following 18 days of continuous combat action its pilots claimed a further 36 Luftwaffe victims, against the loss of only two pilots killed and two Gladiators. On 7 June the remaining 10 Gladiators were successfully flown onto HMS *Glorious* only to be lost with the carrier when she was sunk by the German battleships *Scharnhorst* and *Gneisenau* the next day. All the Gladiator veteran pilots were lost with the ship.

As Britain's army expeditionary force moved to France in late 1939, the RAF detached both bomber and fighter units in support, including 607 and 615 Squadrons of the Auxiliary Air Force by mid-November. These saw their first action against the Luftwaffe on 17 October 1939 when a 607 Squadron Gladiator forced down a Dornier Do 18 off the coast of England; but action over France did not occur until 10 May 1940 when the German invasion of the Low Countries commenced. The Gladiators went into action from dawn that day, and over the following 10 days of unceasing action claimed close to 100 victories (although precise figures will never be known due to the loss of records and so on during the final days of the retreat).

The ultimate sorties by Gladiators took place in various zones of the Middle East throughout 1940–41. On Malta, when Italy entered the war in June 1940, six Sea Gladiators existed and of these a legend was born of a mere trio, dubbed by the UK press as *Faith, Hope* and *Charity* (names *never* used or applied by their contemporary crews, incidentally) which held off overwhelming odds. Gladiators also comprised part of the aerial defenses at Aden, with 94 Squadron, a unit later to fly its biplane fighters in defense of the Iraqi base at Habbaniyah. The last unit to operate Gladiators in the Middle East was 6 Squadron, in late 1941. Outmoded or not, the Gladiators' active combat record during the first 18 months of World War II was impressive by any standards, their pilots claiming some 250–300 aerial victories in toto.

If the Gladiator had been considered an anachronism in modern air warfare, a British biplane of even older conception was to become a legend for its continuous active service throughout 1939–45, the Fairey Swordfish. Derived from an original 1932 Air Ministry specification for a Fleet torpedo-bomber and reconnaissance machine, the Swordfish three-seat biplane first entered Fleet Air Arm service in February 1936, and at the outbreak of war some 14 squadrons and Flights were Swordfish-equipped, mainly in carrierborne squadrons. Subsequently a further 12 squadrons were to fly Swordfishes on operations, apart from numerous small detachments formed for specialized duties. With a maximum speed of barely 140 mph and service ceiling little better than 10,000 feet, the 'Stringbag' – its universal nickname – was distinctly a throwback to 1918 vintage. Nevertheless, it was to achieve undying fame in the annals of aviation during its operational life. Its prowess started on 18 April 1940 when a Swordfish catapulted from HMS *Warspite* bombed and sank the German U-boat *U-64* – the first to be destroyed by an FAA aircraft. For the next six months Swordfish crews undertook a wide variety of hazardous sorties. On the night of 11 November 1940 a total of 21 Swordfish nullified the Italian Navy by attacking Taranto Harbor and crippled three battleships, a cruiser, two destroyers, sank two other vessels, and created havoc among harbor installations – all for the loss of just two Swordfish. This feat was a watershed in the annals of maritime aviation warfare.

Not content to rest on its laurels, the Swordfish added further honors to its battle record throughout the war. In two years of antishipping sorties from Malta, Swordfish accounted for many hundreds of thousands of enemy shipping tonnage sunk in the Mediterranean. In May 1941 Swordfish from the carrier *Ark Royal* crippled the enemy raider *Bismarck* with torpedoes, enabling the Royal Navy to sink the German with gunfire and surface torpedoes. One episode, perhaps even more than the

Taranto triumph, will always be associated with the gallant Swordfish and her crews – the 'Channel Dash' on 12 February 1942. Six Swordfish of 825 Squadron, FAA, led and commanded by Lieutenant Commander Eugene Esmonde, DSO, left Manston airdrome in a desperate attempt to halt the flight of three German capital ships, *Scharnhorst*, *Gneisenau* and *Prinz Eugen*, eastward through the English Channel. All six were destroyed as they attacked, with only five of the 18 crew members surviving. Esmonde, who was killed leading them, was awarded a posthumous Victoria Cross. From then until the close of the war Swordfish crews undertook such a variety of tasks that its battle record reads like a summary of the whole naval war. If the British Navy was there, so were the Swordfish, sinking U-boats, carrying out rocket strikes, escorting merchant convoys to Russia or over Atlantic waters – all were grist to the 'Stringbag's' mill. On 28 June 1945 a Swordfish from the merchant carrier *Empire Mackay* made the ultimate operational flight for the type – the close of a fighting record almost unmatched by any biplane in aviation annals.

Another Fleet biplane – originally intended as a replacement

for the Swordfish! – was the Fairey Albacore, which first reached FAA service in March 1940. Though destined to merely supplement the Swordfish, 'Applecores' – their naval soubriquet – eventually gave some four years of sterling operational effort with the Royal Navy in European waters and especially in the Middle East area. However, the type never surpassed the Swordfish in terms of popularity with crews or overall accomplishments. One maritime biplane which was held in almost equal affection was the stubby little amphibian, Supermarine Walrus. Intended initially as a spotter-reconnaissance aircraft, usually catapulted from its parent ship, the Walrus (or 'Shagbat' to its crews) was issued to the Fleet Air Arm from 1936. From 1939 to 1941 Walrus crews established a dogged record of solid operational prowess on every ocean, but from 1941 it began to undertake a role for which it is now perhaps best remembered – air-sea rescue. The sheer courage and daring of Walrus crews in retrieving ditched Allied crews, often under the very noses of the enemy, became a byword among Allied crews. Antiquated in outline, capable of a maximum speed of only 135 mph at best – and thus easy prey for any

Left: Russia's ubiquitous U-2/Po-2 biplane, designed in 1928, which was produced ultimately in greater quantity than any other aircraft in the world – at least 40,000 machines. This Po-2 was a front-line ambulance in 1941.
Above: Vickers Valentias of 31 Squadron at Peshawar, northern India, in 1941.

marauding Luftwaffe 'hunter' – the Walrus achieved an enviable reputation.

No record of the biplane in World War II could be considered complete in any sense without mention of the aircraft in which almost every Allied airman first learned to fly – the De Havilland DH 82 Tiger Moth. A two-seat, elementary instructional machine, the 'Tiger' came into RAF use initially from 1932. By 1939 more than 1000 Tiger Moths had entered service and during the opening months of the war a number of these were diverted from training duties to Coastal Command. In their 'maritime' role Tigers were used as a 'Scarecrow Patrol' – unarmed spotter aircraft patrolling British coastal waters as a mild form of deterrent against possible German U-boat presence. A total of 8811 Tiger Moths were eventually produced in the years 1931 to 1945. (This figure does not include a total of 420 DH 82b machines converted to become pilotless, radio-controlled 'Queen Bee' aircraft.) Other prewar designed biplanes which gave operational service for Coastal Command during the first two years of World War II included Saro Londons and Supermarine Stranraers. Their retention in front-line units reflected the Allies' concern with protection of the merchant ship convoys conveying vital materials to Britain against the ever-present menace of the German submarine fleet – an echo of 1916–18 when U-boats almost succeeded in blockading the British Isles.

If any biplane could claim a world record for sheer longevity in active use, then the prime contender for such a title must be the Russian Po-2. Designed by the famed N N Polikarpov in 1928, this little two-seat elementary instructional machine – its original role – was destined to be produced in numbers exceeding 40,000. During its extended lifetime the Po-2 has flown in virtually every possible role open to such a design, but first demonstrated its 'teeth' as a war machine when German forces first invaded Russia in 1941. Festooned with small anti-personnel bombs and up to four hand-operated machine guns, Po-2s roamed at will over advancing German troops, using treetop cover, and strafing every target which presented itself.

Left: Fairey Albacores of 827 Squadron, FAA, from HMS *Indomitable*, over eastern Pacific waters.
Right: The 'Stringbag' – the Fairey Swordfish of immortal legend. Though primarily a torpedo-bomber, it was used to carry many other forms of weaponry including, as here, three-inch rocket projectiles.

This day and night offensive soon became a recognized hazard among German soldiery, who nicknamed the persistent little biplanes 'Duty Corporals' or 'Sewing Machines' – the latter referring to the distinct engine sound of the Po-2s. Apart from this direct offensive duty, Po-2 crews (male and female) also undertook bombing raids, spy-dropping activities, ambulance 'mercy angel' missions, night-spotter for the Russian artillery, and a host of pure hack communications sorties. Polikarpov was perhaps better remembered during the between-wars era for his part in designing a number of classic Russian biplane fighters, many of which were to form front-line equipment in the Spanish Civil War and were still on active operations during the opening phases of the 1941 German invasion. Undoubtedly the best-known of his biplane fighters were the I-15 series, first designed in 1933. These first achieved international notice when they commenced combat operations for the Spanish Republicans over Madrid in November 1936, and were quickly nicknamed *Chaika* (Gull) or *Chato* (Pug-nose) by their pilots. Their successes in 1936–38 led the Russians to employ improved variants in the 1938–39 war against Japan. By 1941 the gull-winged biplanes, though ostensibly obsolete, continued their front-line combat against the Luftwaffe with limited success.

The widespread use of overtly outdated biplanes throughout World War II by almost every air force in the world was by no means solely a matter of necessity to fill understrength operational units. During the first years of hostilities, though, such hasty pressing into service of almost any flyable aircraft indicated the blatant failure of past governmental officialdom to recognize the vital need for a strong, modern-equipped air force as the prime form of defense. The eruption of World War II came at a moment in history when aviation generally was only beginning to move into the monoplane age. For example, had the war between Britain and Germany broken out one year

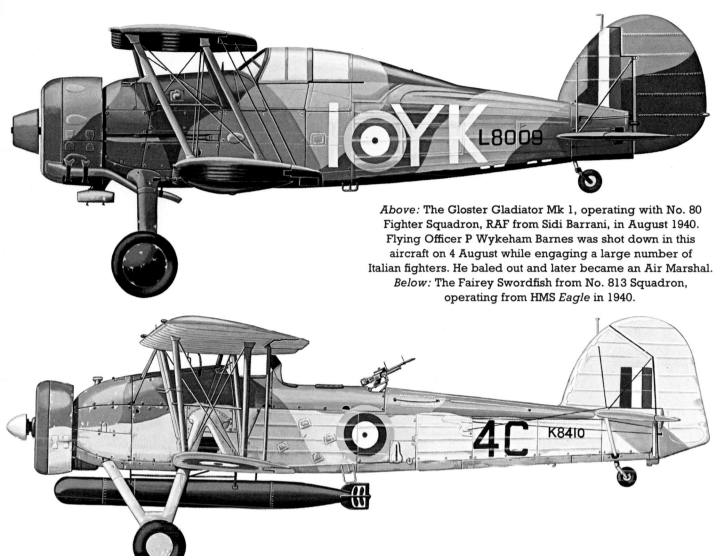

Above: The Gloster Gladiator Mk 1, operating with No. 80 Fighter Squadron, RAF from Sidi Barrani, in August 1940. Flying Officer P Wykeham Barnes was shot down in this aircraft on 4 August while engaging a large number of Italian fighters. He baled out and later became an Air Marshal.
Below: The Fairey Swordfish from No. 813 Squadron, operating from HMS *Eagle* in 1940.

Top left: The famed Gloster Gladiator, now preserved in flying condition at Old Warden Aerodrome, Bedfordshire.
Left: Heinkel He 51B-1 in wartime use as a fighter-trainer.

earlier, at the time of the Munich crisis, the initial phases of aerial warfare would have been fought predominantly by biplanes – at least, until the slowly emerging latest monoplane designs of fighter and bomber had reached wartime production levels for reequipment of the fighting squadrons. Nevertheless, in certain roles the sturdy qualities of a biplane often placed it at an advantage over sleeker, faster aircraft. As a torpedo bomber capable of operating from emergency 'airdromes' such as the crude merchant aircraft carriers, the Fairey Swordfish could hardly have been bettered by any modern monoplane equivalent type. Even in pure dogfighting fighter-versus-fighter combat the superior maneuverability of any biplane often outweighed the greater speed and heavier armament of monoplane opponents, as witnessed by the superb fighting record of the Gloster Gladiator. If further proof were needed of this last assertion, one has only to glance at the combat record of the RAF's highest-scoring fighter pilot of World War II, Squadron Leader M T Pattle, DFC, who achieved almost half of his 41 victories from the cockpit of a Gladiator.

Whatever their role, biplanes gave their utmost in every theater of war during 1939–45. Regarded by younger aircrew generations as ancient in concept, even comical in appearance, and requiring forms of flying almost forgotten in the ever-progressive field of aeronautics, such old warriors gave substance to the cliche 'Old soldiers never die, they only fade away.'

freaks and farces

Right: The Dunne D.5, built in 1910, was a tailless biplane with a single 60-hp engine driving twin 7-foot diameter outrigged propellers. In flight-tests it proved highly stable, and could even be flown 'hands-off' in safety.

Below: The highly unorthodox Edwards' *Rhomboidal* design of 1911. Powered by a 50-hp Humber engine, and ground tested at Brooklands, there appears to be no record of this monstrosity ever leaving the earth in flight.

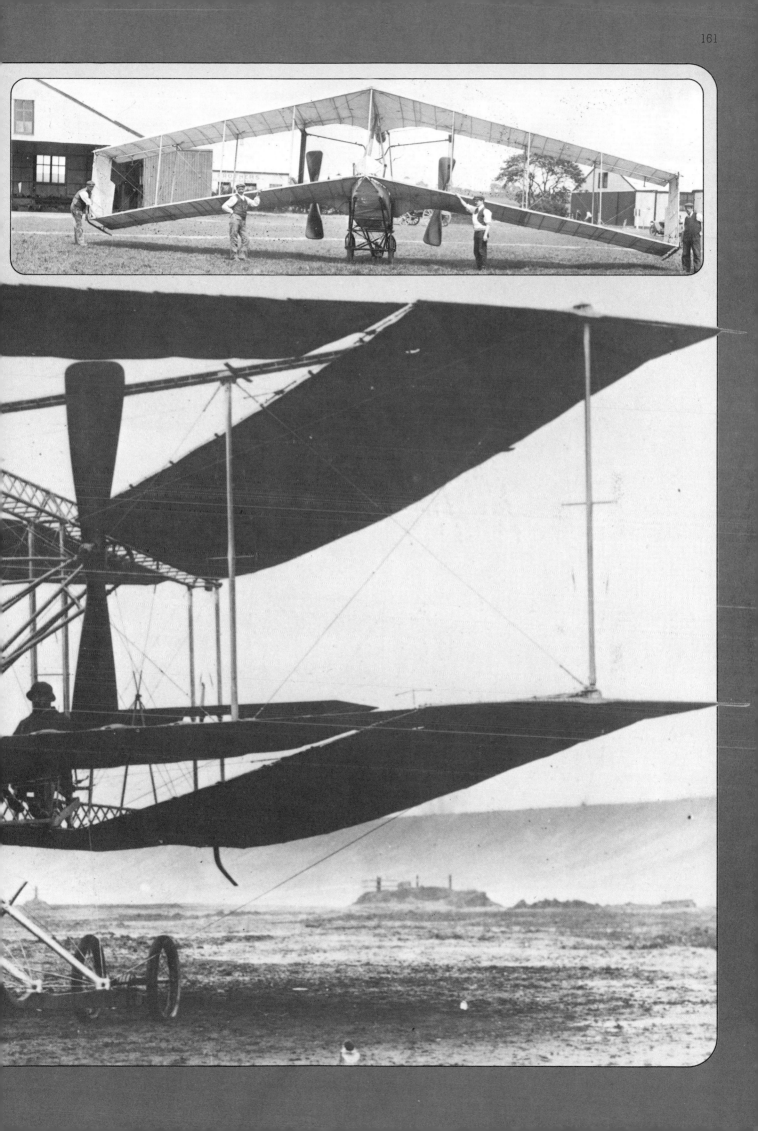

Right: Linke-Hofmann R.I, 40/16, completed in 1917. Its four 260-hp Mercedes engines were 'buried' in the fuselage, driving two outrigged propellers between the wings. Wings spanned 109 feet and its overall height was 22 feet. Wrecked in a crash, the porcine giant was referred to by one pilot as '. . . not an aircraft but a sickness . . . .'

Far right: Wight-built AD 1000 (Admiralty Department Type 1) featured twin slab-sided fuselages with engines in each forward nacelle, with a third engine behind the central crew cabin. Completed in May 1916, its eventual trials proved negative. Only three examples were actually built, numbered 1000, 1358 (illustrated, moored at Felixstowe) and 1359.

Below: Wings galore! The German Oertz W 6 *Flugschoner* of 1916–17 vintage.

Left: Guided missile of 1918 – the diminutive Sopwith Sparrow development of the same firm's AT (Aerial Target), an experiment in radio-controlled aircraft. Its engine was a 35-hp ABC Gnat.

Below left: Nieuport 17, A6686, fitted with triplane wings, presumably in an attempt to improve the pilot's field of vision.

Bottom: Vickers FB 11, a contemporary 'escort fighter' project of the AWFK 12, pictured at Eastchurch on 17 November 1916. Its upper-wing gunner's cockpit required a head for heights.

Right: the production version of the Armstrong Whitworth FK 10 two-seat fighter-reconnaissance, with a 130-hp Clerget engine and single-strut undercarriage.

Left: American ambulance, the Curtiss Eagle transport, suitably marked with the international Red Cross and medical insignia.

Below left: Vickers Type 161 COW-Gun Fighter, in its original form, built to carry a 37-mm Coventry Ordnance Works upward-firing cannon in its nose. First flown in January 1931, it performed well but was not developed further.

Bottom: Intended initially as a 'Berlin bomber,' the Tarrant Tabor was not completed until early 1919 at Farnborough. There, on 26 May 1919, it attempted its first trial flight but crashed before getting airborne, killing two crew members. Its center wings spanned 131 feet 3 inches, and power came from six 450-hp Napier Lion engines.

Right: The Westland-Hill Pterodactyl Mk V was a 1932 variant of several tailless, swept-wing designs tested and modified over a decade. It was envisaged as a two-seat fighter, powered with a 600-hp Goshawk engine, and proved to be fully aerobatic and roughly equal in performance to its contemporary orthodox biplanes.

From the Cockpit

How did it really feel to challenge the winds and dare the elements from a fabric-clothed, wicker-seated, wood-boxed open cockpit, surrounded by vibrating wings and singing wires? How can one recapture the sheer joy of taking to the air in a biplane during its 'golden years'? Or convey the experience of fighting a kill-or-be-killed struggle in aircraft subject to stresses then unbeknown to their designers and constructors? Only the men and women who actually flew during that heyday of multiplane airplanes can truly explain their thoughts, emotions, even occasionally sheer terror, in mounting the skies on manmade wings. If such personal experiences often bear a remarkable similarity in essence, no matter in which era, to each pilot they seemed unique, an inner ecstasy applying solely to the individual. Possibly such heights and depths of excitement and enthusiasm are explained by the relative immaturity in age of a majority of such pilots, reflecting a normal stage in the human aging progression which knows few boundaries in achievement. Yet how then does one explain the same enthrallment felt by ex-pilots in their 'declining' years when given an opportunity to climb toward the sun again in an 'open' biplane – even as a mere passenger – recapturing that inner thrill felt on their first aerial flip?

Among the host of personal accounts of pilots published during the past 70-odd years, a few have succeeded brilliantly in expressing pure emotions in mere printed text. Of these perhaps the following selected examples may serve in small degree to exemplify the exhilaration, the wonder – and the fears – felt by all biplane pilots in all years. Undoubtedly, one of

Above: Colonel S F Cody carefully climbs into the 'cockpit' of his 'Cathedral,' 1914 – a task requiring intimate knowledge of the strongpoints of the machine's construction.
Above left: Two RFC mechanics demonstrate the seating arrangements in a locally modified Sopwith F1 Camel, adapted for dual instruction, at Montrose, 1918.
Below: Seating room in a Halberstadt CL II of mid-1918 – illustrated by this view of a machine from *Fliegerabteilung* 25 – was all contained in a single, elongated cockpit.

Forward visibility for Oberleutnant G Brumowski, the top-scoring Austro-Hungarian fighter ace of 1918, was limited indeed in his Brandenburg D1 'Star-Strutter' Scout, 65.53.

the most memorable occasions in any pilot's life is that on which he or she first takes to the air – the baptism of the sky. Epitomizing the generation of pilots who learned to fly in the first decade or so of man's conquest of the air is the following part-quotation from a letter written to his father by a young Australian, G P 'Bob' Kay, on 8 November 1916. Stationed at the RFC training center at Netheravon, Wiltshire, Kay received his introduction to the flying business in the plywood nacelle of a Maurice Farman biplane pusher.

'It was about 9.30 in the morning when I first went aloft. As the throttle was pushed open, the engine roared louder and louder, and we commenced to run faster and faster across the smooth ground of the aerodrome. It was a beautifully smooth motion, just like a very sweet running car on a good road. You could hardly tell the exact moment that you left the ground. The machine just glided up. We went like this for a few seconds, when the control was pulled back slightly, the machine instantly zooming up as if pulled by a string – a gentle forward movement of the control and we were flying level with the earth stretched 100 feet below, and the passenger feeling just as you have felt when a fast elevator descends suddenly. It is just at the moment of straightening up after the upward rush that produces this feeling. It passes in a moment and you look round on a new world and are dazed with the wonder and beauty of it. Below – far below the roaring engine and vibrating planes – lies the green earth, bathed in the glory of a fresh morning sun. Light fleecy blankets of mist and cloud hide the hollows, and Salisbury in the distance is seen dimly through a veil.

Fields divided neatly by hedges are spread out like a map. Now we are over a farmhouse with its funny little group of toy trees; those white straight lines are roads, and that winding streak of silver melting into the distance is the Avon. It is all very wonderful, and very, very beautiful.

We have now climbed to 2000 feet. Those funny little figures moving about below are Australian Artillery from Larkhill on the move. Just beside that hedge a cavalry picket have tied their horses. They surely are not real horses. Those queer little soldiers and guns are made of lead, and those trees are cut out of cardboard.

Suddenly you find the earth is tilting over – or perhaps it is the machine. One wing is dipping away down and the other is coming up, while your seat becomes almost perpendicular to the earth instead of horizontal. We are turning fast too. You realise vaguely that this is not like being in a car on land, or a boat on the sea – you are in a new element. All this time the air has been rushing past at the rate of 70 mph. It seems the earth is moving and the machine is stationary. This and the roar of the engine help the feeling of unreality.

The controls move slightly and we dip forward, at the same time the noise of the engine ceases. We are coming down. It is a grand feeling sinking easily and swiftly forward and down. As we draw nearer the earth our pace seems to increase – now we are coming straight at a

green field; you can make out the grass plainly. We seem to be moving at a great rate now – surely it is time we flattened out a bit; but we hold on till just a few feet off, when we straighten out easily and gently, the wheels take the ground smoothly, and we run along for a hundred yards or so and stop. We are back on the aerodrome and my first trip in this wonderful other world is over'.

In 1917 'Bob' Kay became a Flight commander with 46 Squadron, RFC in France, flying Sopwith Pups in combat. On 29 June 1917 he died from injuries received in a flying accident over his own airfield. He was buried alongside other pilots of his squadron at La Gorgue.

Cecil Lewis was just 19 years of age in 1917, yet was a veteran pilot in the context of combat flying. He had lied about his age on enlisting in the RFC in 1915, flew FE2b two-seaters and Morane 'Parasol' monoplanes over the Somme battlefields, and was already wearing the purple and white silk ribbon of a Military Cross below the RFC wings on his khaki tunic. In the spring of 1917 he was again in France, a fighter pilot with the renowned 56 Squadron, RFC, flying the first SE5s over the Western Front.

'Rumours of the new SE5 with a 200 hp engine had been prevalent for some weeks, and at last the machine had arrived. I was detailed to take it up on test. I found it faster, and it climbed so well that, since it was a beautiful evening, I decided to find its ceiling.

At ten thousand feet the view was immense, England quartered on its northern perimeter. Oh, to be home again! Just to be over England, even if one could not land on it! After all, why not? I turned north. At twenty-two thousand feet, Kent was below me. Somewhere down there my countrymen were walking, talking, going about their daily business in the peaceful lanes of England. The faintest drift of blue smoke from the chimneys of some country house! There would be the scent of a wood-fire down there, far, far, far below!

The wing-tips of the planes, ten feet away, suddenly caught my eye, and for a second the amazing adventure of flight overwhelmed me. Nothing between me and oblivion but a pair of light linen-covered wings and the roar of a 200 hp engine! There was the fabric, bellying slightly in the suction above the plane, the streamlined wires, taut and quivering, holding the wing structure together, the three-ply body, the array of instruments, and the slight tremor of the whole aeroplane. It was a triumph of human intelligence and skill – almost a miracle. I felt a desire to touch these things, to convince myself of their reality. On the ground they seemed strong and actual enough, but here, suspended on an apparent nothing, it was hard to believe that flying was not a fantastic dream out of which I should presently awake.

From the ground I should be well-nigh invisible. Only the trained observer with powerful glasses would see the minute white gnat five miles up in the profound sky. Only in absolute silence would the faint sound of my engine be audible. They would not know of this brief visit of a homesick man to his native country. To them I was "somewhere in France." I looked long at the island below me, then shut off the engine, and in one long, unbroken glide swept back to France.'

If the hazards of flying were enhanced a thousand-fold during wartime, these simply supplemented a hundred other natural dangers inherited by the pioneer pilots, venturing into an unknown and barely comprehended element in a vehicle of primitive strength and doubtful durability, challenging the awesome might of raw nature. Captain Herbert Reynolds, RE, who had obtained his pilot's 'ticket' in June 1911, set out over Bletchley, Buckinghamshire, in a Bristol Box Kite (50-hp Gnome) on the evening of 19 August that same year. The fine, warm weather seemed to offer near-ideal flying conditions but he soon spotted a black, menacing thundercloud approaching and decided to land rather than run unnecessary risks in view of his modest experience. His own account of what followed is, perhaps, an overt illustration of what came to be called 'pilots' luck.'

'I began a glide but, almost directly I switched off, the tail of the machine was suddenly wrenched upwards as if it had been hit from below, and I saw the "elevator" (*carried on outriggers in front of the pilot*) go down perpendicularly below me. I was not strapped in, and I suppose I caught hold of the uprights at my side, for the next thing I realised was that I was lying in a heap on what ordinarily is the *under* surface of the top plane. The machine in fact was upside down. I stood up, held on and waited.

The machine just floated about, gliding from side to side like a piece of paper falling. Then it over-swung itself, so to speak, and went down more or less vertically sideways, until it righted itself momentarily the right way up. Then it went down tail first, turned over upside down again, and restarted the old floating motion.

We were still some way from the ground, and took what seemed a long time in reaching it. I looked round somewhat hurriedly, the tail was still there, and I could see nothing wrong. As we got close to the ground the machine was doing long swings from side to side, and I made up my mind that the only thing to do was to try and jump clear of the wreckage just before the crash. In the last swing we slid down, I think, about thirty feet, and hit the ground pretty hard. Fortunately I hung on practically to the end and, according to those who were looking on, I did not jump until about ten feet from the ground. Something hit me on the head and scratched it very slightly, but what it was I did not know, for I was in too much of a hurry to get away from the machine to inquire at the time.'

It might be added that despite this uncontrolled fall from about 1700 feet, the Box Kite, which landed on its back, suffered only minimal damage, in itself a tribute to the relative robustness of the design.

Crashes became almost an accepted facet of all flying during the pre-1914 era, as pilots – some barely worthy of the title – sought experience. The war of 1914–18 merely accentuated the casualty rate – in both men and machines – to a point whereby the fatality rate among embryo pilots in almost all air services often exceeded, monthly, that incurred by actual combat conditions. Air crews of all services flew without parachutes until 1918, and even then were only employed by a relatively small proportion of men in the German and Austro-Hungarian air forces. Thus survival in any airplane suffering mechanical defects or, particularly, battle damage was problematical, with the odds heavily weighted against crew survival. Only skill, strength in aircraft construction and – by no means least – a large slice of good fortune offered any chance of living to fight another day.

Hauptmann Heydemarck, an Observer officer of the German *Fliegerabteilung* 17 in 1916 on the Western Front, along with his regular pilot Sergeant 'Take' Engmann, were on a routine reconnaissance flight over the French lines in their Albatros C1 two-seater when they were attacked by a Nieuport Scout in French markings. The combat was brief, with the German crew giving as good as they got in the exchange of fire and eventually forcing the Nieuport to disengage and dive away. The Albatros, however, had suffered bullet damage, including a ruptured emergency fuel tank which soaked the cockpits in raw fuel; just one spark from the open-exhaust engine would convert the aircraft into a flaming coffin. Switching off the engine, Engmann selected a field near Monthois in northern France to make an emergency landing. Heydemarck described subsequent events in detail.

'Our white bird descends in a graceful glide. Now the wheels are touching the ground – but just at that moment the shock of landing sends a vigorous jet of benzine into Engmann's eyes – he is blinded – cannot see the little rise in the ground that lies in our path – bumpety-bump! we run into it – and the way that is still on our machine bounces her into the air again. Quick as lightning it flashes through my brain: ''Bad luck, now we're in for a nasty crash!''

We come down like a log of wood – sideslip over the right wing – ''ratch'' say the spars and ribs of the right wing as they splinter – ''rountz'' says the undercarriage as it cracks off – ''zuck'' says the machine as she goes over on her nose – my hands grip the sides of the cockpit – and the next minute we have turned turtle!

Like a weasel I creep out of the debris. No need to unbuckle my safety-belt – the shock of the crash has torn it apart. ''Take?'' Laboriously he worms his way out of the pilot's seat. His safety-belt has likewise gone to pieces and the shock pitched him against the upper rim of the windscreen. With his handkerchief he tries to staunch the blood running from his mouth and nose, as we silently survey our dead bird. ''Bad luck, Take. I was so bucked with the idea that we would be able to fly home all right!'' Engmann is depressed. ''I put her down so beautifully,'' he says, ''and then I got that damned benzine in my eyes!'' Once again

Pet of an Albatros *staffel* suitably attired, on 9 November 1918.

he wipes away the oozing blood with his handkerchief. I try to console him. "Well, it doesn't matter now. And we had the devil's own luck in our scrap. Just look here – seven hits! Those three in the emergency tank must have passed right between the pair of us. Look at that big hole up there – you could almost get your hand in it. A jolly good thing it wasn't an incendiary bullet!"

But Engmann can conjure up no pleasure at the thought of our victory in the air, for he is still mourning over our machine. "I'll have a squint at the damage," he says. Unfortunately it is severe. The main spar and all ribs of the right upper wing are broken, and the undercarriage can be completely written off. The propeller is a mass of splinters, the exhaust and radiator are bent, while the cockpit is split right across.

Our lovely machine! Machine? No, for us it is no dead piece of machinery but a living creature. We loved our old "griffin" as tenderly as any cavalryman loves his horse. Her graceful form when we approached the aerodrome – her excellent climb when we started off – her speed when she flew us over the front – her lithe movements when we snaked our way through the "Archie" – her agility when we had to get out of an opponent's burst in a fight – the song of her bracing wires when we came back over the front once more – the honourable scars of her bullet holes ringed round with red and black circles – all these things we loved in her.

And now, with a smile of forgiveness, we remembered her faults, her vices and her tricks – how she never liked carrying bombs – how she tried to turn turtle in the clouds – how she never would turn about properly in an air-fight – how she went on strike when we were flying over Chalons – how she refused to let go of the "eggs" we wanted to drop.

And now our good old "griffin" is dead . . . and then *la bête humaine*, the beast in mankind, breaks loose in my soul: "Rather she than we! . . ."

As the aerial war intensified from 1916 to 1918, especially in the context of pure combat in the air, sentimentality for their machines became the least emotion felt by most pilots. It now became simply a vehicle for destruction, a weapon to be used to the utmost capability. The era of the 'dogfight' was now in existence, clashes between formations of single-seat fighting aircraft where no quarter was offered or expected. To survive

was the uppermost thought in most pilots' minds. Lessons in the rock-hard school of fighting experience were empirical; few laid-down 'rules' were available to cope with every possible circumstance. Aerobatic flying, in its crudest form, became the necessity – 'stunt or die' was a common cliche. Man and machine needed to become one if a pilot was to survive, with the actual art of flying reduced to pure instinctive control needing no pre-thought or planning. Airplanes were treated with a harshness of movements which might have horrified the purist pilot but were wholly vital for survival.

John McGavock Grider was an American who came to England in late 1917 for completion of his pilot training, and in May 1918 went to France with 85 Squadron, RAF, flying SE5a fighters under the command of the Canadian ace, Major 'Billy' Bishop, VC. After only a few weeks at the Front, Grider failed to return from a fighting patrol on 18 June. A close friend of Grider's, Elliot Springs, published what purported to be Grider's private diary in the 1920s, though much of the book, titled *War Birds – Diary of an Unknown Aviator*, was in fact written by Springs and provides ostensible 'quotations' from the Grider diary dated long after the latter's death in action. One such 'diary' text at least expresses the authentic thoughts of a fighting pilot over the Western Front in the summer of 1918:

'I have learned many things, especially that discretion is the better part of valor. And in this game, not only the better part, but about ninety-nine percent of it. When there are more than two Huns above you and your immediate vicinity is full of lead, well, my boy, it is high time to go home. Never mind trying to shoot down any of them. Go home and try again tomorrow. How do you go home? You are far in Hunland and you are lonesome. If you put your nose down and run for home you will never live to tell it. All the Huns will take turn about shooting at you until you look like a sieve. These new Fokkers can dive.

Right: The Office – cockpit array of an SE5a in 1918.
Below: Oberleutnant Herman Göring, supremo of the Nazi Luftwaffe, in his Albatros D.V of *Jagdstaffel* 27, 1917.

First you must turn, bank ninety degrees and keep turning. They can't keep their sights on you. Watch the sun for direction. Now there's one on your right – shoot at him. Don't try to hit him – just spray him – for if you hold your sight on him you'll have to fly straight and give the others a crack at you. But you put the wind up him anyway and he turns. Quick, turn in the opposite direction. He's out of it for the moment. Now there's another one near you. Try it on him – it works! Turn again, you are between them and the lines. Now go for it, engine full on, nose down!

Two of them are still after you – tracer getting nearer again. Pull up, zoom and sideslip and if necessary, turn and spray them again. Now make another dive for home, and repeat when necessary. If your wings don't fall off and you are gaining on them, pull up a little. Ah, there's "Archie," that means they are behind you – woof – that one was close – you now have another gray hair – they've been watching you – better zigzag a bit – you can laugh at "Archie," he's a joke compared to machine guns. You dodge him carefully and roll in derision as you cross the lines and hasten home for tea – that is if you know where it is. That is discretion – many a man has gotten out of a fight only to lose to the others who have nothing to do but shoot him down at leisure.'

With the war over, all nations hastily demobilized their airmen, leaving perhaps a tenth of the wartime strength in personnel and equipment. Disarmament was the vogue, backed by political maneuvering toward such an end by idealistic laymen in high places. It was to be at least a decade before governments began to vaguely realize that total disarmament was a pipe dream, and began – albeit slowly – to rebuild strong air forces as a buttress against possible future aggression. A prime example was the British RAF of the 1920s and early 1930s. It was relatively small in quantitative terms, coping with a myriad of responsibilities with obsolescent aircraft, minimal financial budgets, and outmoded concepts for the actual employment of military airplanes, yet the RAF was virtually a model for all air forces. Its stubborn clinging to biplanes as first-line equipment

until almost the outbreak of World War II was not by choice, but its traditions and near-family atmosphere internally led to a reputation by some unknowing cynics as the 'finest flying club in the world.' Frank Tredrey (eventually Group Captain) joined that peacetime RAF as a Halton Aircraft Apprentice – or 'Trenchard Brat,' as these boys have come to be titled – and eventually achieved his one ambition, to fly as a pilot. After several years as a squadron 'driver,' he was selected to go to the RAF's Central Flying School to be trained as a flying instructor. His experiences on this course have been superbly recorded in his book, *Pilot's Summer* (published 1939 by Duckworth, London), an unequalled authentic evocation of RAF flying, and life in general, at the beginning of the 1930s. The following brief extract not only epitomizes the era, but pays an unconscious tribute to Tredrey's patent love of flying, especially in the biplane age:

'There is a happy surprise in store here. In the old days – which ended a few months ago – the (*parachute*) harnesses had two leg straps that came up underneath and snapped on to hooks on front. And you could walk along in comfort with the parachute bumping loosely behind and these two straps hanging loose. When the buckles on the end would clink together and ring and chink with a sweet clear note that was always music to the ear. And to hear it even in imagination recalls by association a hundred other happy sounds and sights and smells. The wump-wump of great all-metal airscrews idling round as row upon row of lean silver snouts already tilt up to the blue and the drifting white cloud armadas. Or the hurried, glittering propeller flicker-nick-flicker as your bull-nosed and squat-tailed little fighter strains squarely against her chocks, all hurry to be off and rip her seven-hundred-horse radial through the air with the pilot hidden somewhere behind it. The smells come crowding in too – the faint, doped drift of silvered fabric, the rich exhaust smell of burnt aviation petrol, the satisfying odour of hot engine metal and oil, and mingled with them all that other smell you notice on playing fields and horse gallops on the downs, clean chalky earth and bruised turf. Flying for a living is the very prince of occupations, and I for one wouldn't trade my heritage for all the messes of pottage in Christendom.

But those were the old days. For everywhere you go now you'll find a different type of harness, the Single-Point Quick Release. All straps come to a metal release-box about as big as your fist, on the chest. The ends snap in and are securely locked by a turn of a round, flat milled plate on front. Then, if you bale out and land in water, one turn of the plate the other way and a smart rap will release the whole lot and you can swim free. No more the music of the clink. Except at CFS, that is. For there, an inland unit never given to flying over water or the possibility thereof, they are using up old stock. And I went away harkening as gleefully as a daft poet to the clink of those buckles again.'

The swan song of the biplane in the military context came during the early phases of the 1939–45 European war. While all participating air forces had a number of biplane fighters and other types on strength for front-line operations – notable examples being the Italian Fiat Cr 32 and Cr 42 fighters in the Middle East campaigns – the RAF's Gloster Gladiator probably epitomized them all with its prodigious fighting record in 1939–41. Just one episode in that brief fighting career may serve to illustrate the Gladiators' doughty qualities, even when facing superior numerical and technical odds. Flight Lieutenant Caesar Hull, a South Rhodesian who had joined the RAF in 1935, was a flight commander with 263 Squadron when this unit returned to Norway in late May 1940 in a foredoomed attempt to resist the occupation of that country by German troops. Their stay was brief, and the furious pace of combat is exemplified by the following extracts from Hull's private diary concerning his own final combats.

'May 26. He (*the wing commander*) explained that the Army were retreating up a valley east of Bodo and were being strafed by Huns all day. Sounded too easy, so I took off just as another Heinkel III circled the aerodrome. God! What a take-off. Came unstuck about 50 yards from the end and just staggered over the trees. Jack followed and crashed. I thought the expedition was doomed to failure and that I had better do as much damage as I could before landing again, so told Tony to land over the blower and set off towards the valley.

Saw some smoke rising, so investigated, and found a Heinkel III at about 600 feet. Attacked it three times and it turned south with smoke pouring from fuselage and engines. Broke off attack to engage a Junkers 52, which crashed in flames. Saw Heinkel III flying south, tried to intercept, and failed. Returned and attacked two Junkers 52s in formation. Number one went into clouds, number two crashed in flames after six people baled out.

Attacked Heinkel III and drove it south with smoke pouring from it. Ammunition finished so returned to base.

May 27. Suddenly, at 0800 hours, the balloon went up. There were 110s and 87s (*Messerschmitt Bf 110s and Junkers Ju 87s*) all around us, and the 87s started dive-bombing a jetty about 300 yards from the aerodrome. Tony's aircraft started at once, and I waved him off. Then, after trying mine for a bit longer, got yellow and, together with the fitter, made a dive into a nearby barn. From there we watched the dive-bombing in terror until it seemed that they were not actually concentrating on the aerodrome. Got the Gladiator going and shot off without helmet or waiting to do anything up. Circled the 'drome, climbing, and pinned an 87 at the bottom of its dive. It made off slowly over the sea, and just as I was turning away another 87 shot up past me and its shots went through my windscreen, knocking me out for a little while. (*NB: Hull had, in fact, been wounded in the head and knee.*) Came to and was thanking my lucky stars when I heard a rat-tat behind me and felt my Glad hit (*his ailerons became jammed*). Went into a right-hand turn and dive but could not get it out. Had given up hope at 200 feet when she centralised and I gave her a burst of engine to clear some large rocks. Further rat-tats behind me, so gave up hope and decided to get down. Held off, then crashed.'

Hull was removed to hospital, evacuated to England and awarded a DFC. On recovery he rejoined his former unit, 43 Squadron, as its latest commanding officer, and destroyed six more German aircraft before being killed in action on 8 September 1940.

Above: The Duchess of Bedford in her DH Moth at Stag Lane Airfield, north of London, 1927.
Above right: Pilot's controls and instrumentation in a Handley Page V/1500 bomber, 1918.
Right: Basic instrument display in the cockpit of an RAF Hawker Fury interceptor in the mid-1930s.

Whether in peace or war, the open-cockpit biplane offered its pilots a communion with nature impossible to parallel in any modern metal enclosed airplane. Let Cecil Lewis, whose awe and wonder of flight has been told earlier, have the closing words from the cockpit.

'There is an experience that every pilot knows. It is a dreadful day, low clouds and rain, and when he takes off the pattern of trees and woods and fields is a dark, depressing tapestry of grey and blacks. The ceiling is down to perhaps 1500 feet. He has hardly time to check his instruments and course before the clouds envelop him. In a second the sombre earth is gone and around him is a featureless cloak of vapour with no horizon, no top, bottom or sides to it. He is suddenly alone, in nothing! Settling down onto instruments he climbs steadily through it, knowing there must be a top, but ignorant of how high above him it may be. The clouds seem to come right into the cockpit, pressing in on him and there is nothing but the roar of the engine and the pointers on the dials. It is oppressive and sometimes terrifying, for curiously enough it requires courage for a pilot to trust his instruments. He feels the aircraft is slipping this way or that, it is turning, stalling, diving. But he knows he must suppress his own instincts and keep everything straight and steady. The bumps throw him about, the aircraft shudders. . . . If he panics, he may fall out of the nightmare in a spin; but, if all goes well, the clouds suddenly turn golden, the blue appears and a moment later he is through!

Through into another world of unimaginable serenity and clarity. The terrible clouds have turned to a level pavement of virgin snow, the heavens are a miraculous vault of blue, crystalline, dazzling, and perfect. Such a fantastic change makes a man want to shout and sing at the glory of it. The sun shines. The shadows of the struts are on the wings. The warmth and light permeate his body. He is alone with the wonder. . . .'

Call Back Yesterday

In an age when man is reaching out into the infinite cosmos of space, seeking contact with planets on the verge of his known galaxy, it may seem an utter paradox that back on earth an international 'growth' industry is afoot both to preserve and refurbish aircraft and vehicles from the earliest years of aviation. Even more intense is the amount of time, money and labor being expended on actual construction of faithful, flying replicas of the aircraft of yesteryear. This near-obsession with the past is not only part of man's inherent nature, but serves a logical purpose. Only by recording and preserving history in such tangible forms can the lessons and examples of a previous era serve as a guide to the future, and – by no means least important – give inspiration for further progress. The conquest of the air has been unquestionably one of the greatest 'leaps forward' of

Above right: **Typical Old Rhinebeck airfield scene – a replica Sopwith Camel, painted to represent the aircraft flown by the Canadian ace of World War I, George Barker, VC, when commander of 139 Squadron, RAF in 1918.**
Below: **A preserved genuine Fokker D VII, in Nazi markings, flown by Ernst Udet in December 1936 in Germany.**

recent years, expanding man's communication with fellow man, and shrinking the barriers of distance and time. It has also added to man's knowledge and understanding of his physical and mental limitations, opening new horizons and possibilities to his inventive genius.

Most nations today maintain aviation museums in some shape or form, though it must be added too many are insufficiently funded or supported by governmental sources and are, in many cases, merely the results of private enterprise and enthusiasm. More than 30 national museums exist today, devoted to the preservation and display of national contributions to the progress of aeronautics. In addition, numerous privately funded aviation collections abound all over the world, backed by even more numerous individual aviation associations and gatherings of sheer enthusiasts, with memberships whose interests embrace every facet of aeronautics and of all ranges of age from octogenarians to adolescents, male and female. Many of these privately organized collections bear the title 'museum' – a title of Greek derivation which originally translated as 'Temple of the Muses,' the Muses being the nine daughters of Zeus, each of whom presided over one of the liberal arts. To 'muse' in the modern verbal sense is to meditate dreamily, a contemplation or reverie state of mind – perhaps an appropriate description of the nostalgic attitude to any museum's contents by its creators and spectators.

Of the world's national air museums, two of the largest are in the United States: the National Air Museum at the Smithsonian Institute, and the US Air Force Museum at Wright-Patterson AFB, some 11 miles from Dayton, Ohio. The latter is also one of the longest established, having originated in 1923 at the old McCook Field, and then moving to the Wright Field four years later. Here can be seen a range of aeronautical exhibits extending from a 1909 Wright-modified Model A 'Military Flyer' – claimed to be

the world's 'first military airplane' – to Mach 4 ramjet vehicles, missiles, rockets and other modern era space 'hardware.' Through all this runs a thread of man's progress through the skies – three-dimensional examples of each major stage in human struggles to conquer the atmosphere surrounding his 'home,' Earth. And the American national trait to study and preserve its past is nowhere better exemplified than in the nationwide fervor for preserving, restoring and reconstructing the classic aircraft of long ago. Such is the enthusiasm, backed with equal benevolence by monied philanthropists in so many cases, that the building of airplanes of the earliest years has now reached almost the proportions of a craft industry. Nor are their constructors content merely to reproduce the aircraft in static form. If a suitable power unit can be found – often original period engines – then the end result is not only as exact a replica of the original design as possible, but it flies! Perhaps no finer example of this urge to go back in aeronautical time exists in the United States than at the Old Rhinebeck Aerodrome, New York. Here the multitude of spectators attending the regular flying days are transported back to the heady atmosphere of the 1914–18 era. The 'background' is of green fields, wooden hangars,

vintage automobiles, ground and air crews often even dressed for the occasion in period apparel. 'Starring' throughout the exhibition are the multicolored flying replicas – scarlet Fokker Triplane, green and yellow Albatros DVa, drab brown Sopwith Pup or Camel, lattice-fuselaged FE8, candy-striped Fokker D VII, and black and yellow checked Avro 504. The smells so beloved of aviation are everywhere – burnt castor oil, fresh dope, gasoline fumes, rubbery fabric aroma. The joyous blip-blip of a rotary engine resounds as its 'host' airplane bumps and sways over the verdant 'airdrome' to take-off point.

Playing with toys? No, this is pure nostalgia in touchable, seeable form, reviving an heroic age in aviation for generations who were born too late to know the biplane as an everyday part of the flying scene. Here is a living representation of all those legendary aircraft and men the younger spectator has only read

Left: De Havilland DH 51, G-EBIR, originally the first aircraft of Kenya's civil register, in 1926, which was given to the Shuttleworth Trust in 1955 and now, fully refurbished, resides at Old Warden.
Below left: A De Havilland 9 bomber of 1917–18 at present displayed in the Musée de l'Air.
Below: The Stearman trainer which was the US air services' equivalent of the RAF's DH Tiger Moth.

or heard about, the steeds in which the 'Red Baron,' 'Black Knight,' 'Mick' Mannock, Albert Ball, Eddie Rickenbacker, and a host of other aces fought and died above the muddied trenches of Flanders more than 60 years ago. These aircraft and their crews had forged a pattern and a tradition from which all later generations were to derive inspiration and the will to maintain that foundation of courage and skill.

In Britain a parallel regard for aviation history is exemplified in several locations. The Imperial War Museum in central London houses a number of historic aircraft types in cramped static exhibition rooms, but has now extended its range to the old RAF fighter base at Duxford. Twenty miles north of London is the relatively new Royal Air Force Museum, with its ancillary Battle of Britain Museum, a monument to the past 60 years of Britain's military air services, their aircraft, men, women and technical artifacts. Further southwest in the lush county of Somerset can be found the Fleet Air Arm's equivalent museum, a practical tribute to British maritime aviation over the past six decades. These are but three leading names among some 40 well-established aviation museums located throughout the width and breadth of the United Kingdom, almost wholly inaugurated by the enthusiasm and determination of men, women, boys and girls, who have sacrificed – if that is not too inappropriate a word – their spare hours, money and labors to

preserve some vestige of Britain's aviation heritage. Nearly all are open to viewing by the public, whose modest entrance fees help to maintain and sustain these splendid examples of individual enterprise.

Perhaps the jewel of the UK aviation centers is a tiny grass airdrome tucked away in the heart of Bedfordshire – the Old Warden Shuttleworth Collection, a sedate title for what is in reality a superb center of aviation living history. Its origins reflect not only a traditional regard for the past, but illustrate overtly what may be achieved by individual efforts unhampered by the blinkers of bureaucratic officialdom. Richard Ormonde Shuttleworth (wealthy grandson of the founder of the Lincoln engineering firm of Clayton and Shuttleworth based at Old Warden Park, near his family home), whose initial hobby was concerned with racing cars, bought a DH 60 Moth (G-EBWD) in 1931 as a private transport. Four years later he was offered two vintage monoplanes, a Bleriot and a Deperdussin, and these sparked off the idea of gathering vintage airplanes in addition to his existing vintage-car collection. By 1939, and the outbreak of war, the aviation collection had expanded in numbers, but he then joined the RAF, only to die in a flying accident at RAF Benson. In his memory his mother formed a Remembrance Trust in 1944 to maintain the vintage collection her late son had cherished, and from this modest beginning grew the present Old Warden-based Shuttleworth Collection.

In order to gather vitally needed finance to support the Collection's aims, the airdrome and its aircraft were opened for public viewing from 1963. Two years later came the first of the now well-known monthly Open Days, occasions when – weather permitting – the Collection's many classic airplanes are not only paraded for spectators' delight, but full flying programs are held. Such days offer the multithousands in public audience an opportunity to see, hear and photograph vintage aircraft in their natural element, the air. With designs ranging from a Bristol Box Kite to the latest jet aerobatic teams – the latter being visiting bonus attractions – such aircraft are in many cases the sole flying example of its type still extant anywhere in the world; for example, the Collection's Blackburn Monoplane is the oldest original British design still flying. Other types seen regularly in the air over Old Warden include Sopwith Pups, an Avro 504K, Bristol F2b, a German LVG C VI of 1918, several of De Havilland's Moth variations, and RAF trainers of the 1930s – Hawker Tomtit and Avro Tutor – alongside that doughty warrior of 1939–40, the Gloster Gladiator. All are maintained in pristine flying condition and carry authentic coloring and marking schemes of their appropriate background.

And what of Europe generally? Here again enthusiasm and dedication know few bounds. In Holland in the Schiphol Airport terminal area is a display of Dutch aviation progression through the years, Fokkers of yesteryear nudging wing-tips with modern jets, biplanes, monoplanes, autogiros – a cross-section of aeronautics, stretching in vintage from 1913 to date. But Europe's largest collection of historic aircraft is tucked away in uncongenial surroundings at the Musée de l'Air at Chalais Meudon, near Paris. It includes a truly astonishing variety of flying machines, dating from an 1895 Lilienthal Glider and several pre-1914 types, through World War I combat aircraft and on into the 1920s and 1930s. The Belgian aviation museum in Brussels is cramped for space but contains several vintage wartime designs from 1914–18. The same conditions apply to various other countries' national collections, in Sweden, Finland, Norway and Austria. Further afield around the globe are parallel collections in Australia, New Zealand, South Africa and even Thailand. Each in its own way proudly displays the aircraft and associated impedimenta which played a national part in advancing the boundaries of aviation both internally and worldwide, a reminder that aeronautical progression over the ages has never been the sole prerogative of any individual nation or species of mankind. As limitless as the environment in

Right: Avro Tutor, K3215, after a long RAF and civil career, joined the Shuttleworth Collection at Old Warden in 1959.
Below right: The Currie Wot single-seat aerobatic biplane originally appeared in 1937, but post-1945 fresh examples were built from original drawings. G-ARZW made its first flights in April 1963, and is pictured here at Gransden in England later.

which it flourished, aviation has always been of an international flavor, each individual effort or segment helping to make the whole.

With few, rare exceptions all such 'national' air museums have – and still – suffered from lack of adequate backing, financially and materially, from the governmental departments of each country concerned. For example, the present Royal Air Force Museum at Hendon, London was *initially* allotted a trifling £3,000 for 'establishment' in the contemporary year's Defence Estimates – a sum which in those days hardly covered the wages of the cleaning staff required! Yet apart from the purely memorial nature of such establishments, lasting epitaphs for the many, many thousands of men who died defending their country's freedom, such museums are the only major method of preserving a heritage of technical ingenuity and outstanding prowess in each nation's aeronautical history. They serve as permanent inspiration for future generations to embellish and extend that heritage. They are intrinsically national monuments to national endeavor, tangible reminders of what was achieved by courageous men and women and a clear pathway for the future.

Such weighty matters are, nevertheless, merely a backcloth to the prime purpose of today's vintage aircraft enthusiasts' international community. To the modern zealot the overriding concern is to produce an airplane which, apart from the pleasure it gave during reconstruction or refurbishment, will help him or her recapture the unique feel of flight during the years of aviation's infancy. It is an emotion unique to flight, a soaring of the spirit of man unmatched in any other field of human endeavor. It was part-expressed by a passenger in a Farman biplane at the world's first international aviation meeting held at Rheims in 1909:

'. . . The ground was very rough and hard and as we tore along at an increasing pace that was soon greater than any motor I had yet been in, I expected to be jerked and jolted. But the motion was wonderfully smooth – smoother yet – and then . . . suddenly there had come into it a new, indescribable quality – a lift – a lightness – a life! Very many there are now who know that feeling; that glorious, gliding sense that the sea-bird has known this million years, and which man has so long and so vainly envied, and which, even now, familiarity can never rob of its charm. But picture if you can what it meant for the first time: when all the world of aviation was young and fresh and untried: when to rise at all was a glorious adventure, and to find oneself flying swiftly in the air, the too-good-to-be-true realisation of a life-long dream. . . .'

Devotees of other, earthbound vintage relics and replicas may claim affinity with such thoughts in other spheres of man's myriad activities, inventions and endeavors, yet the uniqueness of flight is an experience set aside from all others. It is, perhaps, the nearest man has ever come to that ideal of utter freedom of soul and emotion, alone among the boundless vaults of the sky, unimpaired by the petty restrictions of an earthbound existence. Here, and here only, was he, is he, 'the master of his fate and captain of his soul.' To the doubters, let the words of B P Young offer challenge:

'How can they know that joy to be alive
Who have not flown?
To loop and spin and roll and climb and dive,
The very sky one's own,
The urge of power while engines race,
The sting of speed,
The rude winds' buffet on one's face,
To live indeed.'

Left: Fairey Swordfish, the sole flying example of its
type, now part of the Fleet Air Arm Museum at Yeovilton,
Somerset.
Above: A DH Tiger Moth pilot about to start up – epitomizing
every biplane pilot before every 'flip.'

INDEX

GENERAL

AIRPLANES

BIBLIOGRAPHY

The following list of titles from past-published aviation literature is simply a personal selection by this author, intended solely to suggest *some* of the better – in my opinion – stories which evoke an authentic 'atmosphere' of flying in an open cockpit biplane in various eras. A number of these are self-evidently semi-reference tomes, but if certain other titles hereunder strike the reader as unashamed nostalgia or even generous slices of unabashed sentimentality, no matter; it is the sheer joy of flying which comes through primarily. And such heartfelt ecstasy was ever best experienced in a biplane.

The Wright Brothers, F C Kelly. Harrap, 1944
The Dawn Patrol & Other Poems, P Bewsher. E Macdonald, 1917
An Airman's Outings, 'Contact' (A Bott). Blackwood, 1917
Sagittarius Rising, C Lewis. P Davies, 1936
Farewell to Wings, C Lewis. Temple Press, 1964
The Clouds Remember, L Bridgman/O Stewart. Gale & Polden, 1936
Wind in the Wires, D Grinnel-Milne. Hurst & Blackett, 1933
Warbirds, E W Springs. J Hamilton, 1927
I Flew with the Escadrille Lafayette, E C Parsons. Seale, 1963
Flying Section 17, Haupt Heydemarck. J Hamilton, 1937
Double-Decker C666, Haupt Heydemarck. Hamilton, 1938
War Flying in Macedonia, Haupt Heydemarck. Hamilton, 1938
Wings of War, R Stark. Hamilton, 1938
The German Giants, G Haddow/P Grosz. Putnam, 1962
First Battle of Britain, R Fredette. Cassell, 1966
Wings over the Somme, G H Lewis. Kimber, 1976
Recollections of an Airman, L A Strange. J Hamilton, 1938
Early Bird, W G Moore. Putnam, 1963
No Parachute, A S G Lee. Jarrolds, 1968
Sopwith Camel – King of Combat, C Bowyer. Glasney Press, 1978
Winged Victory, V M Yeates. J Cape, 1934
In the Company of Eagles, E Gann. Hodder & Stoughton, 1966
Down Africa's Skyways, B Bennett. Hutchinson, 1932
The Vickers Vimy, P St J Turner. P Stephens, 1969
To the Ends of the Air, G E Livock. HMSO, 1973
Cornwall Aviation Company, T Chapman. Glasney Press, 1978
Planes over Canada, A H Sandwell. T Nelson, 1938
Brackles, F H Brackley. Brackley, 1952
Fall of an Eagle, A V Ishoven. Kimber, 1979
High Speed and Other Flights, H M Scholefield. J Hamilton, 1936
Flying Years, C H Keith. J Hamilton, 1936
The Baghdad Air Mail, R Hill. E Arnold, 1929
Pilot's Summer, F Tredrey. Duckworth, 1939
Flying and Soldiering, R R Money. Nicholson & Watson, 1936
I Wanted Wings, B Lay, Jr. Chapman & Hall, 1937
A Rabbit in the Air, D Garnett. Chatto & Windus, 1932
You are not Sparrows, S J Carr. Ian Allan, 1975
Flying Between the Wars, A Wheeler. Foulis, 1972
Story of the British Light Aeroplane, T Boughton. J Murray, 1963
The Tiger Moth Story, N Birch/N Bramson. Air Review, 1964
The Aviators, W Joy. Shakespeare Head, 1965
The Supermarine Walrus, G W R Nicholl. Foulis, 1966
Find, Fix and Strike, T Horsley. Eyre & Spottiswoode, 1943
The Gloster Gladiator, F K Mason. Macdonald, 1964
War in a Stringbag, C Lamb. Cassell, 1977
Flight Path, F T Courtney. Kimber, 1972
A V Roe, E Lanchbery. Bodley Head, 1956
British Aviation, Vols 1–3, H Penrose. Putnam, 1967–73

ACKNOWLEDGMENTS

Author's acknowledgments
My sincere gratitude goes to the following friends and acquaintances who willingly offered unselfish, ever-ready help in gathering suitable illustrations towards the compilation of this book:
R Athey : Beaumont Aviation Literature : Sidney H Bradd : 'Ted' Hine of the Imperial War Museum : Stuart Howe : Philip Jarrett : Peter Kilduff : G Stuart Leslie : Ken Munson : Stephen Piercy : Harry Woodman. And, in general, to Dave Gray of Walkers Studios, Scarborough, whose skills produced the (usual) superb reproductions of ancient prints suitable for use.

Aeroplane 126/27
Aeroplane via K Munson 50
Aircraft Photographs Ltd 104/05
American Airlines via K Munson 46 (top)
Archiv Schliephake via K Munson 120 (top right)
Associated Newspapers via K Munson 67 (left)
R Athey 10/11, 30/31, 182 (top)
Author's Collection 4/5, 13 (bottom), 15 (top 2), 18 (bottom), 18/19, 20/21, 24 (top 2, bottom right), 28 (top), 28/29, 30 (top right), 32 (top 2), 34 (top left), 34/35, 35 (top right), 36 (bottom), 37 (both), 41 (bottom), 44, 53, 54 (top), 55 (left), 56/57, 62 (bottom), 65, 67 (right), 76, 84/85, 92, 94, 94/95, 96, 96/97, 100, 102, 103, 105, 115 (top), 116 (bottom), 117, 118/19 (all 3), 124/25 (all 3), 129, 134 (left), 138/39 (top), 139 (bottom), 143 (top), 148/49, 150, 155 (top right), 156 (both), 157 (bottom), 158/59, 162 (top), 164 (bottom), 168/69, 169, 170, 171, 172, 176/77, 178/79, 180/81
Beaumont Aviation Literature 62 (top), 134 (right), 144 (left), 166 (top)
BOAC via K Munson 49 (top), 50/51
S Bradd 68/69, 70/71 (all 3), 72 (both), 73, 76/77
Bristol Aeroplane Co 42/43, 135
British Airways 109
C H Claudy Sr 13 (top)
Wg Cdr Elvin 98
Fairey Aviation Ltd 115 (bottom)
Flight 9, 16 (top 2), 16/17, 18 (top left), 54 (bottom), 58/59, 66/67, 88/89, 92/93, 101 (bottom), 106/07 (both), 108 (bottom), 110/11 (both), 116 (top), 120 (top left), 127, 133, 137, 160/61 (both), 174
Glasney Press/M Trim 1
Gloster Aviation 136/37, 155 (top left)
Handley Page Ltd 46 (bottom), 55 (right), 148
Hawker Siddeley Aviation 14/15, 17, 19, 82/83, 89, 90/91, 108 (top), 114, 152 (right), 164 (top)
J L Heard 100/01
S Howe 6/7, 12, 22 (top), 30 (bottom left), 31 (top left, bottom right), 60/61, 64 (both), 87, 88, 151 (top right), 155 (bottom), 158 (top), 182 (bottom), 183, 185 (both), 186/87 (both)
Imperial Airways via K Munson 46/47
Imperial War Museum 36 (top), 39 (bottom), 102/03, 104 (top), 152/53, 173
A V Ishoven 128 (bottom)
P Jarrett 56 (both)
Gp Capt J A Kent 20
P Kilduff 23 (top), 30 (top left, bottom right), 31 (top right, bottom left), 131, 177, 178 (both)
G Stuart Leslie 33, 35 (top left), 41 (top), 52/53, 112, 138/39 (bottom), 139 (top), 141 (bottom), 162 (bottom), 162/63, 163, 164/65, 165, 168
Wg Cdr G H Lewis 38/39
LNA via A J Jackson 63
R Lühr 95
Mann, Egerton Co 39 (top)
MOD (Air) 21, 24 (bottom left), 143 (bottom), 145 (top), 175 (both)
via K Munson 18 (top right), 43 (top), 120/21
K Munson 45 (bottom), 101 (top), 121 (top right), 130, 132/33, 146/47, 151 (top left)
D I Newman 144 (right)
via A W Price 152 (left)
RAF Farnborough 166/67
RAF Finningley 86, 97
RAF Museum 22 (top), 147, 151 (bottom)
Real Photographs 59
Rolls-Royce Ltd via K Munson 79
M Sargent 153
Short Brothers via K Munson 48/49
Siemens Archiv 40/41
C A Sims 86/87, 98/99, 145 (bottom)
Smithsonian Institute via K Munson 123
H Stedman 99
W Stevenson 157 (top)
J W R Taylor 2/3, 7
United Airlines via K Munson 45 (top)
USAF 8/9, 14 (top), 84
US Army 140/41, 141 (top)
US National Archives 90
US National Archives via K Munson 122/23
US Navy 78/79, 112/13, 120 (top left), 128 (top)
R Vann 28 (bottom)
Vickers Ltd 80/81, 166 (bottom)
Westland Aircraft Co 167
G H Williams 34 (top right)
H Woodman 69, 74/75 (both)

Line drawings and cutaways by Mike Badrocke 22/23, 25, 26/27, 29, 32, 130/31, 134/35, 142/43
Sideviews by Mike Bailey 154, 159 (both)
Front jacket Courtesy of Steinhilber & Deutsch Associates, Inc, San Francisco, CA via Christen Industries
Front flaps Author's Collection
Back jacket R Athey
Designer: David Eldred
Editor: Susan Garratt
Indexer: Penny Murphy